The High School of the Future

A Focus on Technology

Edwin T. Merritt

James A. Beaudin

Jeffrey A. Sells

Published in partnership with Fletcher-Thompson, Inc., and
the Association of School Business Officials International

ScarecrowEducation
Lanham, Maryland • Toronto • Oxford

MT

Published in partnership with Fletcher-Thompson, Inc., and
the Association of School Business Officials International

Published in the United States of America
by ScarecrowEducation
An imprint of The Rowman & Littlefield Publishing Group, Inc.
4501 Forbes Boulevard, Suite 200, Lanham, Maryland 20706
www.scaroweducation.com

PO Box 317
Oxford
OX2 9RU, UK

Text design by Andrew Krochko and Brian Russo, Copy Graphics

British Library Cataloguing in Publication Information Available

Library of Congress Cataloging-in-Publication Data

The high school of the future : a focus on technology / Edwin T. Merritt, James A. Beaudin,
   Jeffrey A. Sells.—1st ScarecrowEducation ed.
      p. cm.
   "Published in partnership with Fletcher-Thompson, Inc., and the Association of School
Business Officials International."
   Includes bibliographical references.
   ISBN 1-57886-103-9 (pbk. : alk. paper)
   1. High school facilities—United States—Planning. 2. High school buildings—United States—
Planning. 3. Education—Effect of technological innovations on—United States. 4. High school
environment—United States. I. Beaudin, James A., 1944– II. Sells, Jeffrey A., 1943– III. Title.

LB3209.M46 2004
373.16—dc22
                                                            2003063287

03/17/04 + 1 cd-rom

The High School of the Future
A Focus on Technology

by
Edwin T. Merritt, Ed.D., Director of Educational Planning and Research
James A. Beaudin, AIA, Principal, Education Practice Group
and Jeffrey A. Sells, AIA, Senior Design Architect

Fletcher-Thompson, Inc.
Bridgeport and Hartford, Connecticut, and Edison, New Jersey

with contributions by
Patricia A. Myler, AIA
Richard S. Oja, AIA
Marcia T. Palluzzi, LA

Contents

Part I: Yesterday and Today

Part II: Creating Schools Collaboratively

Part III: The High School of the Future

Part IV: Issues in High School Planning, Design, and Construction

Acknowledgments

Many people contributed their talents, skills, wisdom and experience to this book. First, we would like to express our deep thanks to the principals of Fletcher-Thompson, Inc., for their willingness to support the book's production and their recognition of its importance.

Elliott Landon, Superintendent of the Westport School District, Westport, Connecticut, kindly gave us permission to adapt educational specifications originally developed for the Staples High School renovation in compiling chapter 8, "The High School of the Future: Design Requirements for Specific Curricular Areas."

Fletcher Thompson administrative assistants Marie Fennessy and Joyce A. Saltes provided invaluable help and always found time to help move the project along.

Marcia Palluzzi, LA, developed the database on square footage and the graphical method for presenting the material. She also spent time developing the concept of value engineering presented in this book (chapter 13).

Project Designer Timothy P. Cohen developed the high school of the future concepts and took the time to explain how they function.

The entire Fletcher Thompson Education Practice Group became involved in discussions related to this book and exhibited patience and enthusiasm on many occasions when the book got in the way of revenue-producing work.

Katie Voelker, while a college student employed in a summer position at Fletcher Thompson, read much of the copy, correcting errors and pointing out areas where clarification was needed.

Fletcher Thompson graphic designers Andy Krochko and Brian Russo, with the assistance of Marketing Coordinator Jan Pasqua, deserve our thanks and compliments for their great design and hard work in formatting the book. Marketing Coordinator Diane Kozel was always ready to help with the many details that go into a book's production.

We are grateful, too, for the enthusiasm shown for this project by Managing Editor Cindy Tursman and the staff of ScarecrowEducation, as well as the Association of School Business Officials, and we look forward to continuing our superb working relationship as we bring the other volumes in this series to publication.

And, most important, a large thank-you to James Waller, of Thumb Print New York, Inc., who demonstrated his good humor and editorial skill in scoping the contents of this book, organizing the material, and putting the text into readable shape.

Preface

When a community decides to build a new public high school, it is taking on a task that is sure to be lengthy, immensely complicated, and very expensive. The job of bringing a new high school facility into being is, today, made even more daunting by the fact the nature of education—and especially secondary education—is changing so rapidly.

The expanding role that technology plays in schooling our children is, of course, a major force behind these changes, and in the pages that follow we shall have much to say about technology's impact on education. But technology is not the only driver of change. As policymakers and the American people debate the future course of public education in this country, a very wide gamut of issues is influencing—or *should be* influencing—the ways in which new high schools are conceived, planned, funded, designed, built, and used. These issues, to choose just a few, range from large questions concerning the general approach we should take in educating high school students; to specific questions of curriculum; to concerns about safety in the post-Columbine world; to the pressure exerted on finances and facilities by rising enrollments; to the need to conform to burgeoning federal, state, and local laws and regulations enacted to meet the needs of special-education students; to the desire to define the role that a high school building should play in addressing the facility needs of the wider community.

We at Fletcher-Thompson, Inc.—architects, engineers, interior designers, and educators—plan and design educational facilities. Although the firm is not directly involved in the education of high school students, our long and varied experience in the design of school buildings leads us to understand that each of the issues contributing to the current debate over the future of American public education has—or *should have*—a substantial impact on how schools are designed and engineered.

We say "should be" and "should have," above, because it is our belief that, all too often, this complex of issues is given to little attention in the process by which high schools are planned, funded, designed, and built today. A new high school represents a sizable investment of a community's time, energy, and money, and a community has every right to expect that a new high school building will serve its needs for decades to come. Unfortunately, many high schools being built today—no matter how "state of the art" they may appear—may prove ill-suited to tomorrow's educational requirements. The typical high school being built today is *not* the high school of the future.

There are reasons for this: reasons that are understandable if not, in our view, completely defensible. For one, the process by which new high schools come into being (including everything from board of ed procedures, to state reimbursement schedules, to bond referenda) tends to be weighted in favor of a cautious, conservative approach. It will come as no surprise to anyone that taxpayers are conservative—perhaps the better word would be "prudent"—when it comes to spending money, as frequent defeats of school bond referenda demonstrate. But our research shows that educators themselves—including the Connecticut school district superintendents whom we surveyed in 1999—often display a conservative attitude regarding changes in educational theory and practice and innovation in school-building concept and design (see Chapter 2, "The High School of Today").

Certainly, there is some merit in this conservatism: taxpayers are rightly wary of wasting money; educators are understandably reluctant to support change that potentially threatens to make their already herculean jobs even more difficult to accomplish. But we worry that such conservatism—when it refuses to acknowledge or plan for the far-reaching changes already taking place—may be short-sighted, self-defeating, and counterproductive. By refusing to spend money now, a community may be setting itself up for even greater expenditures in the future. By refusing to entertain alternate design or curricular concepts now, educators may be inadvertently shortening the life span of the school facilities they play a role in planning.

To plan the high school of the future—one that will truly accommodate the educational needs of five, ten, or fifteen years from now—requires a comprehensive *vision*. In compiling this book—which we hope will reach state officials, superintendents and other school-district administrators, local boards of education, principals, teachers, parents, and taxpayers—we at Fletcher Thompson are attempting to begin articulating such a vision. Our point of view is that of designers who have had the privilege of helping to create school buildings across the New England and beyond. But we hope that, by gathering together information on the major issues likely to affect high school design in the years to come—and by outlining a new collaborative process for the creation of genuinely forward-looking high school facilities—we will be providing real, practical help to communities across America that are now engaged in setting their future educational agendas.

——*Edwin T. Merritt, James A. Beaudin, and Jeffrey A. Sells*
Shelton and Hartford, Connecticut, July 2003

Foreword

Think About It *Today*:
The Need for a
Pragmatic Futurist Approach
To School Planning and Design
By Edwin T. Merritt, Ed.D.

We can't stop the future from happening. We're moving into it, every moment of our lives. The future belongs to us, but, more than that, it belongs to *our children*.

These are simple, inarguable truths. So why is it that the future is so often ignored—or given very short shrift—in school planning and design? I can think of several, related reasons.

First of all, it can be *difficult* to think about the future. Not only is the future unpredictable (we all know that), but getting even a limited grasp on the kinds of developments the future might bring requires us to know something about the many trends and forces that are shaping human life right now. That's quite a large field—and so it's no wonder that people feel intimidated before they even begin. Understanding and solving *today's* problems seems challenging enough. Who has the time or energy to think about the future?

Second, thinking about the future can be . . . well, it can be a little *scary*. We Americans are in love with technology; we're thrilled by scientific and technical advances, and we're very quick to welcome the latest innovations—whether they're new features on our cell phones or new gizmos in the doctor's office. But that pleasure is just one facet of what we feel toward technology. Technical advances also frustrate, concern, and—yes—frighten us. The complexity of this emotion is perfectly reasonable. "Technology" doesn't just mean cell phones and MRIs; it means cloning and genetically modified food and sophisticated weapons systems and corporate Big Brothers reading your mind every time you make a credit-card purchase. No wonder our feelings are so mixed—and no wonder that, when asked to think about the future, we so often take refuge in the Scarlett O'Hara syndrome: "I'll think about it *tomorrow*."

Third, planning for the future can seem *expensive,* or financially risky. We sometimes feel that people who want to talk to us about the future are trying to sell us a bill of goods, trying to get us to shell out for costly things that we may never really need—or that will become obsolete before we ever get around to learning how to use them. It goes without saying that this kind of fear—that by thinking about the future, we're opening ourselves up to being taken for a ride—grows more intense during a time of economic instability, when every financial outlay has to be carefully justified.

Finally, thinking about the future can seem *impractical*. For hundreds—perhaps thousands—of years, people have been making predictions about the future that simply haven't come true, or that have come true in ways so very different from what the prophets imagined that it more or less amounts to the same thing. The actual year 1984 didn't look at all like the world predicted in George Orwell's 1949 novel. Y2K was a well-publicized bust, and the year 2001—the setting for Stanley Kubrick's 1968 *Space Odyssey*—passed without any earthling actually engaging in interplanetary travel.

And even when the predictions have been accurate, they've only been partly so. If you'd gone to the "Futurama" exhibit at the 1939 New York World's Fair, you'd have seen the world of 1960 as envisioned by the automakers at General Motors; their vision got some things right—the freeways, the highway cloverleafs—but it also got a lot wrong (the GM folks neglected to mention the rush-hour traffic jams, or the fact that the flight to the suburbs permitted by the automobile would wreak havoc on our cities). Because so little of what I or anyone has to say about the future may come true, anyway—or may "come true" in a way so different from what we envision—why bother to listen?

So, since thinking about the future is so hard, so scary, and so difficult to justify economically, let's not rush right into it. Instead, let's approach the matter "through the backdoor," so to speak, spending a little time thinking about the past and the present—particularly as they relate to the ways we've educated (and continue to educate) our children and to the school buildings we send them to, expecting them to learn.

Backward-Looking Education?

As someone once said, "The past is prologue," and there's no better way to get a handle on the importance of thinking about the future when planning new schools than to examine how well the school facilities built over the past half-century have accommodated the "future." (The future, that is, that's already passed or passing.)

Let's be clear: I'm *not* talking about school buildings that are in bad shape, physically (though there are lots of those, obviously, and there's a crying need for a program of national scope to repair, upgrade, and in many cases replace deteriorating school facilities). I'm talking about *well-maintained schools* in *affluent* school districts. How well have such facilities responded to the great changes that have occurred—technologically and otherwise—in American education over, say, the past 20 years? How well have they adapted to social, economic, and other changes impacting education?

The short answer is: *not* very well.

Let's begin with the very simplest sort of example. The *New York Times* recently reported on a number of Connecticut public high schools that have been forced to restrict the privilege of driving to school to seniors, leaving junior-year drivers grumbling about the indignity—the "uncoolness"—of having to return to taking the bus to and from school each day (Gross 2003). The reason for this harsh new restriction: there's no room for all the cars. This, obviously, is more a social than an educational problem per se, and it's obviously a problem that could only afflict an extremely wealthy society, but it points up something noteworthy. All over the country, high school parking lots are groaning, bursting at the seams from an onslaught of private vehicles—a crisis (of sorts) that these schools' planners and designers never imagined. Snarled traffic has become the norm even at many suburban elementary and middle schools, as parents have increasingly taken to dropping their children off and picking them up rather than relying on the school bus. *Could* yesterday's school planners have anticipated this situation, and taken steps to alleviate it? Perhaps not, but it's certainly an interesting question.

So let's turn our attention to another current space-related issue, one that bears more directly on the educational experience itself. This issue has to do with books. Printed books are physical objects—they take up space. Today, school media centers (which in the days before the "information revolution" used to be known as *libraries*) are, with rare exceptions, designed to store many, many books. They have lots of bookshelves, lots of what librarians call "stack space." So what's wrong with that? We want our schoolchildren to have access to lots of information, right? And doesn't that mean lots of books (and lots of space to store them)?

Well, not quite. Few people seriously doubt that books—printed books—have great value, or that the technology of the printed book, which has been with us ever since Gutenberg, will remain a useful technology for years and years to come. The issue is that, over the past few decades, books—and, for that matter, other printed information sources, like magazines and newspapers—have been supplemented by a wide range of other technologies for conveying and accessing text-based information. *Electronic* technologies.

We all know this. We use these technologies every day. And we know, too, that for many purposes electronic technologies are superior to books as repositories of information. Which is better? A multivolume printed encyclopedia or an online encyclopedia? The "real" encyclopedia takes up several feet of shelf space and gathers dust when it's not being used. It can be physically damaged, and each of its volumes can be used by only one reader at a time. What's more, the pace of advance in scientific and technical fields is so rapid that a printed reference work like this is almost guaranteed to be out of date in certain important respects even before the ink is dry. And obsolescence doesn't just apply to the scientific and technical information such a work contains. Geographical information becomes quickly obsolete (an encyclopedia published in 1991 would have had a long article on the "Soviet Union"). History in all its dimensions—artistic, biographical, cultural, political—continues to unfold, which means that information on the arts, people, governments, and so on all needs to be constantly updated.

A virtual encyclopedia, unlike its tangible, physical cousin, has none of these drawbacks. It takes up no storage space—or not, at least, at the point of access. Its "pages" can't get dog-eared (or cut out); it has no spine to break. It can be used by multiple researchers simultaneously. It can be rapidly and continuously updated. What's more, it can be searched—"mined" might be the better word—for information in a much more thorough, much more creative way than a printed reference work. It can be interactive. And, as if all that weren't enough to convince us of its superiority, subscribing to such an online reference is likely to be vastly cheaper than having to replace that heavy, hardbound printed set every couple of years.

As I say, we all know this. Students today are very much in the habit of taking advantage of electronic resources like the online encyclopedia I've just described (and many, many other such resources besides). *Why* is it, then, that we're still designing media centers to accommodate lots and lots and lots of printed materials? Why are we still dedicating all that valuable, expensive square footage to storage space that, as the years go on, will be less and less necessary?

We all recognize that schools designed even a decade or two ago have in many cases adapted only very uncomfortably to the technological revolution that has so recently transformed virtually every aspect of education. We're all familiar with learning spaces—including media centers—into which computers and other electronic technologies have been "squeezed" in ways that are not very ergonomic and not very aesthetically satisfying, and, most important, in ways that inhibit rather than enhance flexibility. So why do we still design and build new school facilities in ways that probably won't serve future purposes very well?

One reason, certainly, is that we are creatures of habit. We often have trouble seeing the changes that *are* taking place—that *have already* taken place—much less those that lie ahead. We often can't see that solutions to our problems are right at our fingertips.

Let's stay on the subject of printed books for a moment. In December 2002, the *New York Times* carried a story about parents in California and elsewhere around the country who are raising Cain about the weight of all the textbooks that their children are being forced to carry to and from school each day (Dillon 2002). Textbooks have gotten bigger and bigger, heavier and heavier: the story tells of one mother who weighed her daughter's textbook-stuffed backpack, which came in at 28 pounds. Another mother reported that her son's daily textbook burden amounted to 42 pounds. In districts that have eliminated lockers because of concerns about weapons and drugs, the burden on schoolchildren's backs is even greater, since they must lug the books around with them all day long. Backpacks, it seems, are *literally* bursting at the seams; the parents interviewed were of course concerned about the effect of carrying all this weight on their children's long-term health, but they were also angry about the cost of having to replace torn backpacks every few months.

The story mentioned several proposed solutions to the problem: make textbooks lighter-weight; divide them up into multiple (and smaller) volumes; issue students two sets of books—one for use in school, the other for use at home; allow students to bring wheeled packs to school; bring back school lockers in those districts that have eliminated them. What's so interesting here is that the *best* possible solution appears never to have crossed the minds of those parents, educators, and legislators who were interviewed for the story: *Why not just eliminate printed textbooks entirely and replace them with electronic books or other, Web-based products?* The technology for solving the problem already exists, *has* existed for a long time. Why not use it?

Now, granted, there are economic interests at stake here. The publishing companies that produce printed textbooks would have to come up with alternative electronic products. Textbook printers and distributors would no doubt suffer a sharp decline in business. School districts would have to take steps to ensure that each schoolchild could access electronic resources at home. And so on. But changing our basic ways of doing things always has some economic consequences, and in this case it's hard to see how those consequences, as a whole, would be worse than the consequences of what we're now doing—which is virtually guaranteeing that a whole generation of children grows up with musculoskeletal problems resulting from lugging all that weight around.

Now, let's turn our attention away from that old-fashioned technology—paper-and-ink—back to "current" technology (i.e., the computer). Why have I put those quotation marks around "current"? Why, simply because—as we're all aware—computer and computer-related technologies change so quickly that it's very dangerous to describe something as "current." The almost brand-new iMac on which this is being written has a storage capacity of 80 gigabytes—a capacity that would've been unimaginable in a home computer just a few short years ago. What's more, it's networked, wirelessly, to another home computer, a remote printer, and so on. It's perpetually connected to the Internet via cable-TV cable, and access to the Web is virtually instantaneous. Wow, huh?

Well, as you and I both know, such a home setup is hardly unusual these days. And, if you're reading this five or even two years hence, you're probably not thinking, "Wow!" You're probably thinking, "Gee, what a puny little machine. And what a primitive little network!"

I'm hardly trying to brag about how "wired" (or "wirelessly wired"?) I am. The point I'm working toward is that—knowing all we do about the rapidity of change in the arena of computer technology—we continue to design schools for *today's* technology (or even yesterday's), not tomorrow's. There are, of course, some new schools that have been designed in technologically savvy, future-oriented ways, but there are plenty of others whose design is based on the "state of the art" of five or even ten years ago. Face it: Hard-wired computer stations and dedicated computer labs—no matter how well integrated into an overall design—begin to look positively antique in an era when students are carrying cell phones and PDAs that enable them to connect wirelessly, effortlessly, and oh-so portably to the Internet.

In fact, we're not even fully exploiting the *wired* technologies that we have. In many cases, high school science-lab suites are still being designed in ways that don't realize the space- and cost-saving possibilities conferred by virtual laboratory environments—which are now quite sophisticated, highly interactive, and every bit as good for teaching the experimental method, especially in the lower high school grades, as their "real life" equivalents. And we're certainly not utilizing distance-learning and teleconferencing technologies (which already exist) to the fullest extent possible, which would allow schools, districts, regions, and even statewide school systems to share resources more effectively, cutting costs and (probably) enabling space reductions in individual schools.

I should go a step further, here, and say that it isn't at all difficult to imagine the space-related implications of a situation in which all of a school's students (and faculty, and staff) have immediate, personal, wireless, fully portable access to a full range of electronic information resources. This kind of situation—and we're not very far from getting there—would, very simply, eliminate the need for the various sorts of dedicated computer spaces that are still being designed and built into new schools today.

Parking lots. Printed books. Information technology. So far, I haven't even touched on the core aspects of the educational experience—the curriculum itself, the instructional methods used, socialization dynamics, the ways schools are organized (and the ways they make decisions)—or on how these central aspects of education, as they exist today, do or do not relate to today's and tomorrow's realities.

I've just been reading an intriguing little book (you see, I do appreciate the value of paper-and-ink technology!) called *Tomorrow Now: Envisioning the Next Fifty Years,* by futurist Bruce Sterling. Let's listen to Sterling's tren-chant take on contemporary American education and its relevance to the world outside the schoolhouse. "My older daughter," Sterling writes

> is a student in high school. . . . [S]he lives in harsh paramilitary constraint. She has a dress code. She fills out permission forms and tardy slips, stands in lines, eats in a vast barracks mess room. She comes and goes at the jangle of a bell, surrounded by hall monitors. . . . My child leads a narrow, tough, archaic working life. Though she isn't paid for her efforts, she'd do pretty well as a gung-ho forties-era Rosie the Riveter. . . .

Today's schoolchildren are held to grueling nineteenth-century standards. Today's successful adults learn constantly, endlessly developing skills and moving from temporary phase to phase, much like preschoolers. Children are in training for stable roles in large, paternalistic bureaucracies. These enterprises no longer exist for their parents. . . .

Today's young students are being civilized for an older civilization than their own. . . .

It's no coincidence that my daughter is appalled by her schoolwork but thrilled by the Internet. Loathing her official school assignments, she spends hours tracking down arcana on the Net, in patient orgies of pop-culture research. (Sterling 2002, pp. 42–44)

Now, certainly Sterling is exaggerating for effect, and he's generalizing from his own child's experience—or his impression of it—to make claims about the experience of all schoolchildren in America today. I'm an educator, and so I know that there's lots that's right about American education, and that conditions in many schools aren't nearly so harsh or so "archaic" as Sterling would have us believe. But, even so, the overall point he's making has some real validity. The enforced routines his daughter is made to follow in school are backward-looking; they have precious little to do with the world outside school—or with the workworld she'll ultimately enter. That workworld's values include an extremely high degree of flexibility, intensive teamwork, the ability to think and act effectively "on your feet" and in "nonlinear" modes. The contemporary and future workworld is (and I'll use a big word here) *protean*—as is the valued employee in that world of work. "Protean" means constantly changing, constantly shifting, constantly *adapting*—and nothing could be further from the inflexible, regimented routines that Sterling's daughter has to endure.

It's clear that that backward-looking approach to education *has* to change.

A Critical Juncture

American public education has reached a critical juncture in its history. The trouble is, the situation is confusing, and no one really knows which of several directions we'll eventually end up moving in. It's likely, in fact, that we'll continue moving in several different directions simultaneously. Let me give some examples.

On the one hand, a concern for diminishing performance in reading, math, and science skills is leading us, as a nation, toward greater standardization in curriculum, with an emphasis on evaluating every schoolchild's performance—and that of every school and school district—through standardized testing. This approach, epitomized in the No Child Left Behind Act passed by Congress and championed by the Bush administration, has its virtues—it demonstrates real concern for academic excellence—and it has many advocates.

At the same time that there's this push toward standardized curricula and standardized testing, however, there's a movement in what seems to be the opposite direction: toward highly exploratory, individualized (and individually directed) learning. There are, for example, teachers, parents, and students across the country who are railing against the practice of "teaching to the test," which, in their view, sucks the life (and a great deal of the value) out of the educational experience. There's the gathering strength of the middle school movement—treated in great detail in another volume of this "Schools of the Future" series—which has always emphasized a highly exploratory, highly interactive educational experience for young adolescents. There's the fact that advances in learning and information technologies make it possible, as never before, to individualize curricula *while* making sure that individual students' performance matches or exceeds standards. (I'm talking, here, about sophisticated "data warehousing"/"data mining" systems that enable an individual student's performance to be plotted against school-wide, district-wide, statewide, and national standards as well as against that student's own past record. Such systems foster the development of individualized curricula that closely attend to students' academic strengths and weaknesses.)

Then there's the growing importance in American education of what's called "multiple intelligences" theory, which emphasizes that children have different gifts, different inherent abilities, and which stresses the need to recognize these differences when designing curricula and instructional methods. And the multiple-intelligences movement, with its emphasis on adapting educational technique to the ways in which children actually learn, dovetails with another trend—that of applying the lessons of neurological science to instructional methods and even to curriculum itself. MIT professor and popular science writer Steven Pinker, whose books describing how the brain works have been bestsellers, is, like futurist Bruce Sterling, very concerned about our schools' failure to adequately prepare children for life outside the classroom. In a recent *New York Times* op-ed piece, he takes American schools to task not only for teaching the "wrong" subjects (he thinks all students should receive basic instruction in economics and statistics, for example), but for teaching *in the wrong way*—that is, by neglecting to apply what science has learned about human cognition to what goes on in the classroom (Pinker 2003). The connection between neurology and education is one to which I'll return, below.

Finally—and perhaps most important—there's the unstoppable movement toward greater *choice* in American public education: the growing number of magnet schools, charter schools, and other "alternative" (theme-based and specialized) schools that are offering parents real alternatives in how their children will be educated.

What's so interesting about this current, conflicted situation—in which "standardization" vies with "experimentation"—is that there *are* ways of making these competing, seemingly divergent, approaches come together. One of the ironies of this critical juncture is that some "alternative" schools—magnets, charters, and others—whose instructional methods, curricular approaches, and modes of organization are *anything but* "standard" may offer the greatest hope of improving students' performance according to standard measures. Magnets, charters, and other specialized schools—highly attentive to the needs of individual school-children and specific populations—stand, in many ways, at the cutting edge of American public education. Alternative schools' potential to transform American education for the better is being increasingly recognized: in February 2003, for example, the Bill and Melinda Gates Foundation—which is turning into one of the most important "movers and shakers" on the American educational scene—gave a grant totaling $31 million to fund the startup of 1,000 new alternative schools across the country (Winter 2003).

Not all such schools are successful, of course, and the jury is still out regarding whether, for example, the charter school movement will live up to its proponents' promise to revolutionize learning, but it is clear that the best magnet, charter, and other specialized schools are doing something that too many "traditional" schools are failing to achieve: they're actually preparing their students for the world—including the workworld—outside the school doors while at the same time ensuring that they "measure up" academically.

Future Schooling—*And* the Future School

At this point, you may be asking yourself what any of this has to do with the school buildings—the physical places—in which we educate our children? The short answer is: *plenty.*

I've described a present-day situation that is, at best, confusing, and I've begun outlining a future in which, it seems, the only certain thing is *change.* Given these realities, it's pretty clear that the most important, overriding principle in school design should be *flexibility.* If a learning space is likely to be used *both* for the traditional, "stand and deliver"–type instruction best suited for preparing students for standardized tests *and* for more exploratory forms of learning combining large- and small-group interaction and individual research, then that learning space *must* be flexible in order to succeed in both its purposes. If, as seems certain, new learning, information, and other technologies are going to continue coming "on line"—and if, as also seems certain, these technologies will quickly be adopted by public schools—then it is *absolutely essential* that schools' learning spaces and infrastructure be designed to flexibly accommodate them.

When you look at the future this way—focusing on the inevitability of change and, therefore, on the need to flexibly accommodate it—"futurism" turns out not to be a flight of imaginative fancy but rather a very pragmatic approach, indeed.

Keeping that in mind, let's take a look at some of the other changes that the future is likely to bring to American education. Some changes, of course, are likely to be expansions or extrapolations of current trends: Because educators increasingly recognize that the performing arts are great tools for building leadership capabilities and fostering the kinds of interpersonal dynamics that enhance teamwork and democratic decision-making, schools of the future are likely to contain a greater variety of (technologically sophisticated) performance spaces, or spaces that can easily be adapted for performing-arts purposes. As everyone grows increasingly conscious of the impact of the physical environment on learning, the indoor-air and acoustical environments of school buildings are likely to be of higher and higher quality. As the manifold benefits of environmental/sustainable, or "green," design become clearer, multiple aspects of a school's interior and exterior environments are likely to be shaped with green-design principles (which cover everything from energy efficiency, to recyclable building materials, to indoor environmental quality) in mind. And as concern grows over increasing rates of childhood obesity, the wholesale retooling of school food programs, with an eye toward balanced nutrition, becomes inevitable. When compared with upcoming technology-based changes, however, these sorts of developments appear tame and relatively uncontroversial. We don't have any trouble envisioning them, and, in fact, we welcome them optimistically and with open arms.

We need to keep that openness and optimism handy when looking at some of the technological advances that lie ahead. Some of the developments discussed below, if and when they are proposed and/or implemented, are likely to be highly controversial and are sure to set off heated debates. But because technology continues to develop so rapidly, I think it's high time that those debates begin, so that the technology-based changes that are introduced into public education result from truly democratic decision-making involving American society at large.

If we don't think about these things now, we're *not* being pragmatic; in fact, we run the risk of letting the future determine us, rather than vice versa.

Human/Computer Interactivity

Even as we prepare this book, the media tell us of successful human-brain chip implants that help disabled people by restoring or simulating sensory abilities, enabling them to function better and more completely by supplementing the brain's power with computer power. It's easy to imagine this kind of technology being more widely applied—for instance, in the form of "remedial reading [or math] chips" implanted in the brains of students with certain kinds of learning disabilities. Such an application would, I think, represent a marriage of education and neurological science like that that Steven Pinker proposes. (And—who knows?—such chips might even eventually enable ordinary human beings to communicate "telepathically," merely by thinking and directing their thoughts at others.)

In a similar vein, voice-activated technologies—in which spoken commands generate computer responses—are a reality today, assisting people with disabilities, those who suffer from repetitive stress injuries, and people who must keep their hands free for non-keyboard tasks. (The 2003 Honda Accord automobile features just such a voice-activated, interactive navigation system.) It strikes me that such technologies naturally lend themselves to educational uses, and that, far from merely "responding" to spoken commands, computers—with whom students will communicate wirelessly—may actually play a role in directing the educational process.

For instance, when the full range of personal data on each student is "warehoused" on school and family servers, the computer will "know" enough about the student to respond to questions such as, "What question *should* I have asked?" The answer will, in effect, control the direction the student takes. As this kind of artificial intelligence advances, it's interesting to speculate about the kinds of answers computers might give to philosophical or spiritual questions. Will the home system give the same kinds of answers as those provided by the school computer? How will school systems deal with church-state questions, and how will parental rights be protected? We don't know the answers to these questions. In fact, we don't even know whether they're the *right* questions—but we can predict with some certainty that this kind of high-level human-computer interactivity will set off some heated debates.

Biotechnical and Genetic Technologies

Interactive technologies like those just described may be supplemented by biotech and genetic technologies that enhance mental and physical performance. I can certainly envision the day—perhaps not too distant—when genetic blueprints of each student are available to educators (and their computer "assistants") to help them determine students' inherent strengths and weaknesses and to design individualized educational programs on that basis. I can even foresee educational prescriptions—for both mental and physical activity—being regularly updated (perhaps even daily) through ongoing analyses, conducted in school-based labs, of students' blood chemistry. A changing regimen of dietary supplements and drug therapies would be prescribed to modify and control the changes in students' biochemistry and to prepare students for optimum educational experiences.

(If nutritional programs were individualized, you can just imagine how the cafeteria environment might be altered!)

In such a scenario, computers would be involved not only in prescribing dietary/pharmaceutical regimens but in monitoring each student's well-being and measuring and assessing the progress he or she makes. As information was collected, the computer would make the necessary adjustments to the prescription, and teacher/facilitators would monitor the computer-student interaction and intervene when appropriate. "Guidance counseling" would come to include mental capacity mapping, sense acuity diagnostics, and the monitoring of brain and overall physical development informed by an intimately detailed understanding of the student's genetic makeup.

The facility-related impacts of these trends are likely to be extensive—involving, for example, the expansion of today's nurse's suites into small-scale, comprehensive diagnostic and treatment centers, and the transformation of physical education spaces into banks of individual workstations equipped with smart machines that use genetic and biochemical data to help individual students maximize physical performance.

Let's not underestimate the importance or scope of the changes that will be wrought by advances in biotechnical and genetic-engineering technologies. Futurist Bruce Sterling, who devotes a chapter of *Tomorrow Now* to the coming biotech revolution, writes that "Biotech is by no means tomorrow's only major technology[,] . . . [but] if it survives and flourishes, it will become the most powerful" (Sterling 2002, pp. 5–6). So, in thinking about schools of the future, let's try to think about what a school in which educational and biomedical functions are intertwined might look like.

We're making a mistake if we don't at least try to anticipate such changes. Schools designed 30, 20, or even a dozen years ago didn't anticipate the explosion in social, support, and technical services that are, today, commonplace features of the educational environment (I'm talking about everything from ESL labs, to planning and placement teams (PPTs), to onsite social workers, to IT support). The result? A situation in which such services are squeezed—uncomfortably—into facilities not designed to accommodate them.

Security, Scheduling, and Environment

Security technology is currently being revolutionized by so-called biometric devices, which "read" and store handprint, fingerprint, and retinal patterns—or even scan and remember human faces—and that permit or disallow access based on whether a person's biometric attributes match those in the security database. Inevitably, biometrics will come to be used in school security systems, providing a much higher level of access control than is possible with the card-access and other, similar systems in wide-spread use today.

These technologies will reinforce the attitude that the school community is a family, supported by the school's safety and security system. All the members of the community will be connected to one another, and, in effect, the community will protect itself. "Bubbles of caring" will invisibly surround school facilities so that security personnel will be alerted instantly when a problem arises. The technology for this kind networkable system—in which security is based on individual alert buttons worn by all staff and students—already exists and has been implemented at some colleges.

That "bubble of caring" will embrace scheduling, as well. It's more than conceivable that the standard school day will become a thing of the past. As learning programs are increasingly individualized, it will become less and less necessary for all students to arrive at and depart from school grounds at the same times each day. With computerized scheduling and navigational systems in place, there would be no reason why school bus routes couldn't be highly individualized, too, with students being picked up from home, delivered to school, and then taken back home or to after-school activities as their individual schedules require. (In fact, such a system could make sure that the efficiency of a fleet of buses is maximized, potentially leading to reductions in the number of buses needed to serve a school's student population.) Moreover, if students were required to wear or carry chips connecting them to the Global Positioning System, their whereabouts could be constantly tracked and monitored. (Another option would be to surgically implant such chips—making it impossible to lose a student or for a student to elude authority—but this sort of procedure would surely be greeted by outright hostility by some members of the public, making its introduction controversial, to say the least!)

In the school building itself, computers will control the interior environment—not just to modulate comfort conditions as necessary, but also to alter aesthetic characteristics of the environment. We can foresee a day when the colors of walls, floors, and ceilings; images projected on walls; and the amount and quality of light in interior spaces are all controlled by computers, which will change the colors, images, and light as changing educational and recreational activities warrant. On a gloomy day, a ray of artificial (though natural-looking) "sunlight" might stream through the atrium skylight; the mood of a dismal winter afternoon might be enlivened through the projection of a lush lawn onto the floor adjacent to a wall showing a virtual waterfall.

And technology is likely to alter the school environment in another way, as well. Throughout the "Schools of the Future" series, we often speak of the trend—in all public school facilities—toward increased after-hours use of the school building by the larger community. Pursuing that trend further, we can envision a time when educational facilities become even more tightly interwoven with the overall governmental and institutional life of the community. As data resources and support services become ever more intertwined (and instantly, virtually accessible), and as land for municipal construction projects becomes ever more costly (and less readily available), a time may come when it makes a great deal of sense to consolidate many or all municipal functions—governmental, recreational, health, and educational—on a single campus.

The School as "Laboratory"

Whether or not any of the particular changes discussed in the preceding sections is ever implemented, it's clear that technology will continue to radically transform the educational experience. And one of the most sweepingly important aspects of this transformation will be that education—at all levels from preschool on—will become increasingly "experimental" and laboratory-like. Not only will students be in increasingly constant virtual communication with electronic resources, but the seamless interplay between computers and their human users will enable an educational approach that is individualized, problem-solving–oriented, and "experimental" in the best sense of the word. This will be true in all schools—but some magnet, charter, and other alternative schools are even now on the cutting edge of this transformation.

No longer will experimentation be confined to the science lab. Instead, a school building's learning spaces will become all-purpose laboratories in which hands-on and virtual experimentation of many different, interdisciplinary sorts can be carried on. Students—employing personal digital assistants (PDAs) that combine MP3, DVD, cellphone, and laptop computer functions in a single device—will communicate with electronic resources containing vast amounts of information. Wall-mounted "smartboards" will replace blackboards/whiteboards in classrooms and other learning spaces, making even the traditional, lecture-style format a much more interactive experience. Through empirical experiments and heuristic thinking, students will continually be testing the truth and viability of their parents' and teachers' assertions and creatively evaluating the workability and wisdom of schools' organizational structures.

Experimentation, of course, is an ongoing, never-ending process. It involves dialog, the back-and-forth of argument and counterargument, the openness and flexibility required to change one's mind and alter one's direction. It involves interaction—and, of course, interactivity is the foundation of a healthy democratic society. Advances in learning and information technologies don't mean very much—they aren't very valuable—unless they support and extend our ability to work together to find solutions to the challenges besetting us. Education doesn't mean very much—isn't very valuable—unless it prepares our children for the life that awaits them outside the school's doors.

And this, finally, is the earmark of the school building of the future: that it not only enables students to learn interactively, but that it actually nurtures the dynamics of creative, positive, solutions-oriented interaction. It does this in all sorts of ways, from incorporating interactive technological resources into every dimension of learning; to articulating space in ways that enhance human-computer, one-on-one, small-group, and large-group interaction and democratic decision-making; to ensuring that the environment enhances rather than impedes learning.

Does all this sound scary? Well, change always is at least a little scary, and designing facilities to flexibly accommodate change while ensuring that change is for the better is scarily daunting.

But let's not be frightened. To respond effectively to the changes the future may bring, we must ourselves be willing to change our thinking, our strategies, and our priorities. This is a potentially endless task, and one that

Introduction:

A Vision of the Future High School

we—as designers, educators, parents, and citizens—should welcome. Let us, together, begin thinking about the future *now.*

A recent draft report on redefining high school graduation requirements issued by the Connecticut Department of Education puts the matter bluntly: "The future is now. It is time for change to ensure that Connecticut students are prepared to live in a new era . . . . Any delay puts . . . high school students at risk of failure in this fast-changing world." (Department of Education 2000)

The desire to provide high school students with an education that, in the words of the report, is "more challenging, rigorous, appropriate and relevant" is hardly unique to Connecticut. Educators across the country feel the need just as urgently. Nor is the transformation of the high school experience just a matter of curricular reform. To effect the kind of far-reaching change that the authors of the Connecticut report recommend, we must fundamentally re-envision the environment in which new kinds of learning will take place. For unless high school facilities are themselves transformed in ways that truly serve the new approaches to secondary education now being considered and implemented, the success of those approaches may be compromised.

The future is now. That doesn't mean, of course, that the future is clearly visible. What it does mean is that, unless we begin, right now, to think about what the future is likely to bring—and unless we base our thinking on the best information we have about forecasted technological advances, developing social and cultural trends, and probable economic, political, and environmental realties—we won't be able to respond to the unpredictable demands with which the future presents us.

This book is intended to acquaint readers with some of those advances, trends, and realities insofar as they are likely to alter the nature of public high school education in America over the next decade and beyond. The questions guiding our research and speculation are simple ones: How can we design a school building today in such a way that it will further—not hinder—the new approaches to high school education now being discussed or put in place across the country? How can we make certain that the facility itself will be as adaptable—as capable of responding effectively to change—as the more flexible organizational structure and educational program it is meant to house? How can we ensure that a new high school building will easily accommodate the technologies on which the new educational approaches depend? How can the building foster a climate in which each student is safe, feels that he or she is cared about, and knows that he or she is receiving the best educational experience that the community can offer? And how can the facility itself participate in community-building by serving the educational, recreational, cultural, and even governmental needs of the wider community?

In Part I of this book, we look briefly at the high school of yesterday to show how dramatically facility needs have changed over a mere quarter-century or so, and then we examine the high school of today—taking into account information gathered in a recent survey of school-district superintendents—to point up some of the plusses and minuses, adequacies and inadequacies, of the typical high school planning and design process as it currently exists. Part II focuses on collaboration—the key to successful planning, design, and project management. The centerpiece of the book, Part III is a meticulous exploration of the high school of the future, including a discussion of general principles guiding design, specification guidelines, and a series of conceptual diagrams and visual tools. This is followed, in Part IV, by a detailed look at some of the many issues (political, financial, practical, aesthetic) that now influence—and that will continue to influence—the creation of high school buildings.

But, first, let us turn our attention to the overarching question: How do we go about envisioning the high school of the future? In the remainder of this introduction, we discuss some of the essential factors that should guide our basic rethinking of the planning, programming, design, and use of high school buildings.

A New Educational Philosophy

More than any other, one factor drives the need to re-envision high school facilities: the brand-new approach to high school education that is now being discussed, experimented with, and, in some cases, broadly implemented in states across the country. This new philosophy has several major components:

First, it focuses on the need to create *individualized programs of study*. This approach—represented, for example, in the Connecticut Board of Education draft report cited above—relies in part on recent psychological research demonstrating that different people (whose brains and senses differ) learn differently. For learning to be effective and efficient, programs of study must reflect and serve these highly individualized differences—"multiple intelligences," as they're often called.

But the approach equally depends on a common-sense awareness, developed through long experience, that today's typical high school curriculum—in which, with rare exceptions, students are lumped together in classrooms and shuttled through very similar programs of study geared toward meeting fairly rigid graduation requirements—fosters an environment in which too many students are bored and apathetic, too many "fall through the cracks," and too high a dropout rate is sustained from year to year. By contrast, a curriculum that maximizes individualization challenges *all* students to become actively involved in their own education, enabling them to ask—and answer—questions like the following:

*   What am I really interested in?
*   What do I want to do in life?
*   How do I get there?

In other words, under this approach we're no longer saying to the student, "Here are the hoops you have to jump through in order to graduate." Instead, we're saying, "Here's what you want to do. Let's work together to see if you can do it!"

As programs of study are individualized, the role of the teacher fundamentally changes—from that of presenter and evaluator to that of *counselor and facilitator*. This is a far-reaching change, and one that, admittedly, can only be gradually introduced if we're not to overwhelm our high schools' already overburdened faculty. On the other hand, this basic transformation of the teacher's role has the real potential to make high school teachers' jobs *more* pleasurable, not less. Consider the difference between having to "manage" a class of bored 16-year-olds, some of whom are disruptive (which, all too often, is what the current classroom experience amounts to), and being able to get deeply involved in helping students set, prepare for, and achieve their educational goals. Which of these options would most teachers find the more attractive? (Needless to say, to work at all, the large-scale implementation of individualized learning *must* be supported by appropriate and effective technology, which we discuss below.)

Next, the new philosophy of high school education emphasizes *collaborative learning* and a *problem-solving* orientation. For years now, businesses (architects and engineers included) have used terms like "teamwork" and "solutions" in marketing their services. These may be "buzzwords," but they're not empty of meaning. Far from it: a collaborative and solutions-oriented approach is *crucial* to a business's effectiveness and success. Just as relevant is the fact that the maintenance and improvement of American democracy and democratic institutions depend utterly on people's ability to work together to find solutions to the large challenges facing us. Problem solving and creative collaboration are critical to the world of work *and* to participation in our democracy, and a high school curriculum that ignores the development of these vital skills imperils individual students' chances of success *and* the very fabric of democratic decision-making.

Individualized programs of study and collaborative learning aren't contradictory—they're *complementary,* and the high school of the future, to fulfill its mission of adequately preparing students to enter the worlds of work, higher education, and adult social and political life, must accommodate both. Doing so involves a considerable re-evaluation of how space is designed and how it is used. The classroom isn't about to disappear—in fact, individualized study and collaborative group process will be built on a solid base of learning achieved in more traditional classroom activities. Even so, the typical high school of today—whose "egg-crate" arrangement of classrooms continues to closely resemble the high school of yesterday—poorly serves these new kinds of learning experiences. Re-envisioning the high school building *doesn't mean getting rid of the classroom* (though classrooms themselves will be configured much more flexibly than they are now). Rather, it involves *expanding* the variety of spaces and functions the facility houses.

A third major component of the new philosophy of high school education involves the need to instill in all students *a lifelong passion for learning*. In a sense, of course, this is not a new value: educators have long stressed the importance of seeing education as an ongoing process—one that continues long after an individual has completed formal schooling. But a person's need to develop the attitudes and skills necessary for pursuing learning constantly over the course of his or her life is intensified in an era of inexorable technological change, in a world where long-term job security is a phenomenon of the increasingly distant past, and in a society where people are living longer and remaining active and healthy much later in life. For financial success as well as for self-fulfillment, a never-ending desire to learn is the essential key.

In practical terms, the high school of the future serves this need for lifelong learning by opening its doors to the wider community. High school isn't just for high schoolers any longer. Community college satellite centers (offering "grades 13 and 14" to qualified high school students as well as those who have graduated), adult continuing education programs, senior centers—all these have a place in the high school of the future. And, even now, municipal governments across the country are joining with local school district administrators to investigate ways of permitting the wider community to take advantage of the sophisticated information technology with which high schools are being equipped—for instance, by making the high school media center a branch of the local public library system and designing rules and schedules that permit everyone to access its resources.

A High School "Without Walls"

Sophisticated information and telecommunications technologies underlie and support virtually every aspect of the high school's transformation. In a later section of this book ("Technology Utilization," chapter 14), we examine in some detail the impact that technology is likely to have in shaping and sizing spaces inside the future high school and on its grounds. But, to start, let us sketch in a broad-brush fashion some of the many ways in which

technology will influence school-building design—and, relatedly, some of
the ways that new educational concepts and approaches will define how
high schools take advantage of technology.

In some important respects, the high school of the future is a school
"without walls"—and one without rigid, universally applied schedules. The
advent of the Internet and the World Wide Web, the not-to-be-contained
explosion of resources available on line, the ability to access intranet
resources via the Web from remote locations globally, the increasing
sophistication and functionality of wireless communications, the instant
availability of an increasingly voluminous virtual library of electronic
books—all these and other technological developments mean that certain
courses of study can be effectively pursued *anywhere, anytime.*

As individualized programs of study come to account for a greater and
greater share of any high school student's overall curriculum, it becomes
less and less important that every student be inside the high school
building, following a set schedule for a set portion of every weekday. The
high school, of course, retains its essential importance as *the* place where
certain kinds of learning experiences happen: in-person conferences
between the student and the teacher/counselor; classroom instruction and
face-to-face collaborative problem-solving; distance-learning classes that
require sophisticated video-teleconferencing equipment; hands-on experimentation in higher-level science labs; and visual and performing arts,
industrial arts, and physical education. But many individual projects can be
just as efficiently—perhaps *more* efficiently—performed outside the
building's confines: at home, on a family vacation, at a workplace where the
student pursues a school-approved job or internship, while abroad in a
foreign exchange program. (Obviously, the possibilities are vast.)

Individualizing programs of study requires individualizing schedules to
facilitate those programs' differing requirements. A student who's pursuing
an individual program designed specifically for her might, for example, spend
part of a given "school day" at home, studying an individually assigned text
or preparing an essay; then travel to school to attend a class, go to band
practice, work in a language lab or in the media center, and/or meet with
other students on a collaborative science project; then go off to an afternoon "school-to-career" internship with a local employer. Not only would
her schedule differ from those of her classmates, but their schedules would
all differ from one another's.

It's important to emphasize that this vision does *not* involve any lowering of
standards—either of academic performance or of behavior. It may be feasible
to consider tracking students' whereabouts through the use of chip devices
linked to the satellite Global Positioning System—the same system that, for
example, allows friends and relatives to monitor runners' progress in the New
York City Marathon. (The same chip-driven system could also allow
students to keep abreast of their own ever-changing schedules.) And

students' progress in individualized courses of study would be gauged from the frequently updated information stored in the district's data warehousing system. (Such systems are described below).

As the chapter on "Technology Utilization" (Chapter 14) explains at greater length, the chip and networking technologies that make individualized programs and schedules possible are also likely to have substantial, measurable practical benefits for schools themselves. For instance, if all students carry lightweight laptops capable of instantly downloading course materials and electronic textbooks from a school district's intranet (eliminating the need to carry heavy textbooks to and from school), and if students, because of individualized schedules, arrive at and depart from the high school building at different times of day, it becomes thinkable that we could entirely eliminate lockers—replacing them with a checkroom in which coats and other items could be stored until needed. (The differing arrival and departure times would prevent "rush hour" crushes at the beginning and end of a school day that would make the checkroom option unworkable.) As any high school administrator knows, getting rid of lockers would eliminate a host of safety and security problems—and, besides, would have a significant beneficial impact on new school buildings' first costs.

Likewise, students' differing schedules—coupled with powerful information technology that keeps close track of where every student needs to be, and when—may allow school districts to substantially reduce their fleets of school buses. Explained in more detail in the "Technology Utilization" section, such a system would permit a school-bus driver to know who needs to be picked up and taken to school (or vice versa) and the times of day at which those students must arrive at school or home—and then to customize the bus's route depending on that day's needs. Because students would be coming to and going from school all day long, the mass arrivals and departures of the current system would be eliminated (meaning that school bus parking lots could be greatly downsized). And because buses would operate all day long, the number of buses in a fleet could be sharply cut—perhaps by as many as half.

Technology's impact on educational spaces *inside* the school building will be just as dramatic as its effect on the high school careers of individual students. Not only do new technologies (and the new kinds of learning patterns they support) foster the creation of new kinds of educational spaces, but they also have a significant impact on the size and configuration of traditional spaces, including (for example) classrooms, labs, storage rooms, media centers, medical suites, and so on. For instance, when all students attend school equipped with laptops capable of wirelessly accessing the district's intranet and the World Wide Web, classrooms no longer need to contain banks of computer stations for online instruction.

The "Technology Utilization" chapter speculates on some other specific effects of technology on spaces inside the school, but one of our conclusions there is especially significant and should be mentioned up front: the increasing use of sophisticated communications technologies may result in our ability to reduce the square footage now typically allotted to many classrooms, labs, and media centers—perhaps by as much as 20 percent off some spaces. This, we think, will come as a bit of relief to boards of education now faced with seemingly inexorable increases in the square footage a new high school must contain.

Data Warehousing/Data Mining

Decision-making in the high school of the future—whether those decisions are about an individual student's program of study or about improving a school's or district's overall performance—will absolutely require a system of data storage that is easily accessible and capable of responding quickly and meaningfully to the sometimes complex questions that educators pose.

To help a student make the right decisions about his or her individualized program of study, a teacher/counselor has to have immediate access to that student's records (and all the indicators of progress they contain). But to accurately gauge the success of the individualized program, the teacher/counselor must also be able to compare that student's achievement—for example, on standardized tests—with school-wide, district-wide, state, and national data. Similarly, to institute effective (school-wide or district-wide) reforms in areas ranging from curriculum, to scheduling, to facility utilization, to test administration and beyond, principals and superintendents need rapid access to a vast array of data—*and*, more important, they need an information management system that will allow them to ask complicated questions and be given usable answers within a reasonable time frame. Such systems—"data warehousing systems," as they are known—have been around for some time, but they're only now becoming affordable enough for school systems to employ.

"Haves" versus "Have-Nots"

Any discussion of the use of technology in public schools seems inevitably to raise issues of the "haves" versus the "have-nots." In public school systems that are already riddled with inequities—so this important question goes—doesn't the "technologization" of education create even sharper differences between rich and poor districts? Doesn't it widen the gulf between affluent students' chances for success and those of low-income students?

A convenient, though not very satisfactory, answer to this question is that such differences will tend to level out over time, as more and more people—at all income levels—acquire and use advanced communications technologies. After all, television sets, which 50 years ago only the relatively wealthy could afford to buy, are now ubiquitous in American homes. And more recent communications technologies—VCRs, cellphones, DVD players, and (of course) personal computers—show even faster rates of adoption and use across the income spectrum. The problem with this kind of answer, of course, is that it refuses to address the very real inequities in funding that less-wealthy school districts continue to endure or the comparatively limited access to powerful communications technologies that students from low-income families have.

There is, in fact, a much better way of responding to this concern—which is that government is working, right now, to level the playing field. Under the e-rate system made possible by telephone-bill surcharges introduced by the federal Telecommunications Act of 1996, billions of dollars have become available for poorer urban and rural districts to spend on education-related high technology. Few are the underfunded school districts that haven't already taken advantage of this program. Most cities, for example, have already instituted take-home computer programs in their schools—programs that benefit not just the students themselves but also their parents, who are encouraged to get involved in their children's "high-tech" learning. This isn't to say that the "haves versus have-nots" problem doesn't exist any longer, but it does mean that our society has traveled some distance on the road to solving it.

Technology: Some Hidden Costs

Technology, unfortunately, breaks. Computer networks crash. Equipment malfunctions. Systems that are set up improperly don't work as they should. And when adequate time and money are not spent on training people—administrators, principals, teachers, staff—to use new hardware and software, these all-too-common problems grow worse.

These are hard realities for school districts, which are being forced to employ a growing army of information-technology specialists to fix the problems that so frequently arise with the systems presently in use. What's more, districts are in fierce competition for IT talent; in general, the private sector can offer those with technical problem-solving know-how much better wages than public school systems can afford to pay. And to make matters even worse, the "hidden" costs of maintenance, repair, and training are sometimes underestimated or not fully acknowledged by budget-makers, who tend to categorize technology costs in capital fund and tech department lines. Taking all these things into account, a very scary question rears its head: As the amount of sophisticated technology used in schools grows, aren't these problems likely to become even worse—ultimately touching off a crisis?

Well, the problems are certainly real and the costs high: it's estimated, for example, that at the beginning of this decade Connecticut was spending upwards of $300 to $400 per year per student to support the technology that already exists in its schools. But it's also the case that states and school districts—sometimes in partnership with private companies and philanthropic organizations—are beginning to explore ways of meeting the challenge.

First, it's being recognized that technology isn't the province of the tech department alone—and that other categories of employees, given the right training, are perfectly capable of operating and maintaining portions of a school's overall technology system. At one Plainville, Connecticut, school, for example, a receptionist (whose job category falls under the budget line for secretarial employees) received training and was able to serve as the school's webmaster. The potential for this kind of "crossover"—in which "nontechnical" staff assume responsibility for technological systems' operation, upkeep, and at least some simple repairs—is even more apparent and natural in other employee categories: for example, media-center staff. It's safe to suppose that, as time goes on, the boundaries between the techies and the non-techies will grow fuzzier and fuzzier, with a larger and larger sector of the school community helping to run the systems and make sure that they remain in working order.

Moreover, there's no reason that students themselves shouldn't play a part in making sure that their school's technological systems run smoothly and well—and do so while receiving valuable training that will help them land well-paying technical jobs after graduation. At many high schools, traditional industrial-arts "shops" are being supplemented by classes in computer-system repair, and several major computer-industry companies have inaugurated programs in which they donate equipment to public high schools for use in classes where students learn how infrastructure works and how to maintain and repair it.

Community Celebration and Commitment to Students

Before turning to chapter 1, "The High School of Yesterday," we want to conclude this introduction by returning to the issue of the school building itself—by briefly exploring two themes that, we feel, should be major factors in shaping the design of the high school of tomorrow: *community celebration* and *commitment to students*.

State officials, local boards of education, building committees, architects and engineers—all the people involved in the planning and design of a new high school—need to attend closely to the high school's evolving role as *the* place where a community comes together to celebrate the achievements, talents, and joys of all its members. A visionary imagining of the future high school requires an awareness of the many ways that this potentially very versatile facility—which is probably also the most expensive public facility a community will undertake to build—might serve the wider community. We've already discussed how the high school of the future can, and should, be designed to support lifelong learning. But to this must be added the need to size auditoriums generously enough to accommodate community music, dance, or theatrical events; "town hall"–type meetings; and community awards ceremonies. Likewise, entrances, exits, and pathways through the building—as well as vehicular traffic patterns and parking lots outdoors— must be planned in ways that *invite* the community into the school while providing adequate security theft, vandalism, and injury.

We even think it's worth considering designing the future high school around a "Main Street" concept—one that provides a central gathering place where, say, the whole family could meet after school hours, perhaps to share a meal together before each member goes off to pursue one or another of the many activities the building might be hosting that evening: a jewelry-making class, aerobics training, a seminar acquainting senior citizens with the social services available to them.

This is not to forget that the primary responsibility of those who participate in the planning and design of the high school of the future *is to the students who will learn there*. Architectural and engineering elements have a great bearing on students' safety, comfort, and sense of well-being. For example, a decision to maximize the use of low-maintenance, vandal-proof building materials (terrazzo floors, ceiling tiles that can't be punched-through, graffiti-resistant rough stone finishes on both exterior and interior walls) will not only save a district money in the long run by reducing maintenance expenses, it will also foster an environment in which students take pride. (And experience clearly shows that damage begets damage, and that clean, graffiti-free, well-maintained school environments tend to stay that way.) Quality lighting systems that don't create glare or interfere with computer screens, ample natural light and architectural features (atriums, glass walls) that underscore a sense of openness, facility-wide air conditioning that supports year-round activity—these and other elements all facilitate learning and demonstrate a community's investment in its children's school lives.

But by "commitment to students" we also mean a commitment to *overall design excellence*. In our long experience as designers of school buildings, we at Fletcher Thompson have often noted a reluctance on the part of boards of education and building committees to consider base-building design that's even slightly adventurous or forward-looking. The reasons for this aesthetic conservatism aren't hard to sympathize with. Adult decision-makers, nostalgic for their own younger days, sometimes feel strongly that a new high school should look "like high schools did when I was in school."

And local leaders are often intent on inculcating longstanding, time-tested values—and they understandably worry that a school whose design is too "radical" might seem disrespectful of its context.

Granted, all of the changes—in curricular reform, in technology utilization, and so on—that we've been discussing in this introduction *can* be accommodated within a high school building that, from the outside at least, resembles high schools of the past. But we choose to close this introduction with a question—one that we mean to be provocative: *Wouldn't high school design that's less traditional, more future-oriented, better demonstrate a community's commitment to its children and to the world that they will inhabit?*

Don't worry. In raising this question, we're not proposing a wholesale abandonment of traditional architectural values. But we are, we hope, saying that truly successful high school design—like all good design—is comprehensive; that it explores the complex interaction of exterior and interior space; that it exploits, as appropriate, the aesthetic potential of new building materials. That it delights the eye, and moves the soul, and inspires.

As will be clear from the first chapter, no one really wants high schools of the future to *be* like yesterday's high schools. So is there any necessary reason why they should take their architectural cues from the past? True, the high school of the future will be a magnet for the entire community. But its primary users will be young people. Why not design for them?

Part I : Yesterday and Today

Chapter 1

The High School of Yesterday
by Edwin T. Merritt, Ed.D.

In the early 1970s, when I was superintendent of the Monroe, Connecticut School District, we expanded and renovated the town's only high school, Masuk High, which had originally been built in the mid-1950s. As I look back on that experience, I have to pause in wonder over how much has changed in less than three decades—both in American education and in the kinds of expectations that a community brings to a high school facility project. Here's what it was like back then:

The like-new renovation and expansion (for a projected enrollment of 1,250 students) was fairly typical of moderate-cost high school renovations of the era. Of course, that the planned improvements and enhancements were rather limited doesn't mean that they immediately met with the community's approval. The flat, built-up roof; the motel room-style HVAC system; the vandal-proof ceiling tile—each of these elements was criticized as being lavish and too expensive, as was the spread out, ranch-style, everything-on-one-level plan. (The original building was one level, but it was thought by some that building on top of that level might be cheaper than expanding the one-level arrangement.) Though all these things ultimately made it into the renovation, the local taxpayers' association mounted arguments against each.

In the final plan, an open-air smoking area was situated next to the front door (the aim was to reduce the amount of cigarette smoke in the building). The lobby opened into an administrative complex at the left, a cafeteria on the right, and, at the center, a circular hall junction leading to classrooms, the auditorium, and a large and highly visible industrial arts complex. A full array of shops was constructed in the old gym, with large display cases for wood and metal shop projects viewable from the front entrance.

Access to town water was two miles away through rough terrain, so the taxpayer group assented to a swimming pool complex, since the pool could double as a rather large fire extinguisher.

Things went wrong, of course. The vinyl tile proved difficult to polish; the roof required a great deal of maintenance; the HVAC system was difficult to balance, and, as for the smoking area and the industrial arts complex—the culture changed, and these components soon lost their allure.

What's even more surprising from a present-day perspective, though, is how little thought was given—and how little provision made—for a whole host of elements and strategies that would naturally be included in any such renovation today. No attempt was made to air condition the building, for instance, and there was very little effort to segregate certain spaces to make them more accessible for community use and continuing education.

Even back then, there was some discussion about the need for collaborative learning space and for a wiring system for computers, but no action was taken. Egg crate–style classrooms prevailed, and the need to plan for technology was met by the installation of a computer lab. The media center, which looked out on an interior courtyard, did include a pit and reading center (designated by a circular pattern of brick and carpet), but there was little effort to make it a space for real collaboration.

The administrative organizational structure was simple: one principal's office, including space for two assistant principals. There was no discussion about reorganizing the school according to a "house" system. There was no attempt to provide offices for departmental chairs, even though the need for such spaces existed. The head of the physical education department and the athletic director were given office space, but no attempt was made to provide an exercise room. Fine arts spaces included a large art room, a choral/instrumental room, and a relatively well-equipped auditorium that could seat up to two classes (approximately 600 students) at once.

The circulation pattern in the building was a long loop. No attempt was made to integrate departments of study or to provide for interdisciplinary activity. There was no provision for a large, centralized forum space, and very little space was allocated for parent-teacher conferences. In a magnanimous gesture to the taxpayer association, however, three rooms at the back of the building were made available for use as a senior citizen center.

The list of deficiencies—at least from a present-day perspective—goes on and on. The 1970s renovation of Masuk High School included none of the following:

- An energy efficiency strategy

- Recycling of waste (an incinerator was used)

- Seasonal boilers

- Spill-proof oil tanks

- Adequate parking for students' cars

- Teacher office space

- Conference rooms

Moreover, no thought whatsoever was given to ensuring disabled access to program areas. In fact, a wide variety of items called for in today's code requirements were simply missing from the newly renovated school.

HOW THINGS HAVE CHANGED!

In 2000, the Monroe District prepared for a second renovation of the 50-year-old Masuk High School. The school's wish list looked like this:

Priority 1

- Teachers' resource rooms
- Classroom expansions
- Screens and "blackout" shades for classroom windows
- TV/VCR in every classroom
- HVAC improvements
- Increased electrical power supply
- Copier rooms
- Nurse's room expansion

Priority 2

- Conference rooms
- Computer networking labs
- Language labs
- New carpeting
- A fiber-optic cable infrastructure
- A weight-training room addition to the physical education department
- An expanded cafeteria (for fewer "waves")
- Technologically up-to-date chemistry lab
- Modern lavatory/plumbing
- New library furniture

- Parking/traffic control

- Air conditioning

Priority 3

- Increased number of spaces for support services (e.g., social workers' offices, psychologists' offices, and associated conference rooms)

- Storage rooms

- Art room expansion

- Better corridor lighting

- Technology enhancements/improvements (e.g., data warehousing, electronic bulletin boards, high resolution monitors in classrooms for Internet image display, etc.)

- Main office/guidance office expansion

- Music wing/new auditorium

- Disabled-access code compliance

Priority 4

- Computerized auto repair shop

- Whiteboards

- Replacement rubberized (outdoor) track

- Small theater

- Student publication room

Priority 5

- Expanded greenhouse

- Auxiliary gym

- Self-contained, on-site alternative school

- Tennis courts

- Psychology lab

- TV production room

- Satellite

- Expansion of band/chorus rooms

- Security office

- Keyless entry

- Smart/debit cards for cafeteria

- Teachers' workstations

A list like this embodies several agendas, including the creation of a year-round educational environment, that weren't even dreamed of in the mid-1970s. And many of the items—including space for counseling and collaborative learning, expansion of the fine arts program, and new technology to provide information and security via connectivity—are hallmarks of the educational specifications of the future.

Chapter 2

The High School of Today

The high school of today is a bit like the Roman god Janus—the one who looks forward and backward at the same time. This "betwixt and between" situation results from a variety of forces, some driving change while others apply the brakes.

On the positive side, the good economic times of the past decade have, to some extent, encouraged leaders to accelerate change by focusing on the following facility-related areas:

- Creating a learning environment that facilitates collaboration and problem-solving

- Implementing disabled-access code standards

- Encouraging environmental education and interests

- Fostering increased parental involvement and community use

- Accommodating continuing education, particularly grades 13 and 14

- Accommodating performing arts needs and interest

- Facilitating democratic discussions by school and community

- Accommodating projected enrollment increases and special student needs

- Providing infrastructure for today's and tomorrow's technologies

- Facilitating the use of individualized learning prescriptions

At the same time, however, the process by which new high schools are planned, designed, and built—and the climate in which this process occurs—are resistant to change and are weighted in favor of conservative solutions that may not adequately address future needs. These forces, which make the environment a very difficult one in which to propose or effect fundamental change, include the following:

- Relatively low levels of state reimbursement (and inequities in state reimbursement). State formulas, which focus narrowly on square footage requirements, simply do not allow reimbursement for anything other than a basic structure. Building elements that go beyond the basics are put on the school district's "tab"—that is, they will not be reimbursed—and are therefore subject to intense scrutiny by the voters. When referendums occur, intense debate focuses on issues such as income tax–property tax equity and overall taxpayer burden, and proposed projects are often defeated.

- The call for a focus on basic education still occupies center stage, and related taxpayer referendums ensure that program and design recommendations will be conservative.

- In states like Connecticut, local-control theory still holds strong sway over legislative decisions, minimizing statewide control in the areas of school-year calendars, salary schedules, and curriculum/testing/competency mandates. Architecture usually mirrors this attitude by producing relatively traditional structures reflecting local preferences. There is relatively little room for change, creativity, and innovation.

- Construction contracts are low-bid oriented, making it difficult to spend more money to achieve higher quality. Environmentally friendly building materials, superior HVAC systems that produce higher indoor air quality, and sophisticated security devices and systems cost more than most building committees want to spend. Educational technology installations and those energy conservation measures that can be funded, at least in part, by rebates are exceptions to this rule. But even here there are problems: for example, technology infrastructure installations that qualify for federal "e-rate" discounts are popular, but many districts fail to apply for the funding in a timely way.

The conflict between the old and the new comes to the fore even in the ways that individual schools and school districts "deal with" technology. For example, today's students walk into their high schools with cell phones, beepers, CD players, and laser pointers, and some even park motorized scooters in their lockers. Educators all too often respond by making and enforcing policies against the use of such equipment in school. For the moment, the fact that we are just at the beginning of struggles over emerging technology—and that we will have to find ways of using students' own technology (cell phones, laptops, PDAs) for educational purposes—escapes the rule-makers.

Meanwhile, the prevailing situation, in which opportunities for change conflict with a process that supports the status quo, exists during a time when *the need for new school facilities is at a peak*. In Connecticut as in many states, high schools are anticipating significant increases in enrollment over the next decade, with an enrollment plateau expected around 2008. School districts need lots more high school space, and they need it very soon. Options include renovations, renovation/expansion combinations, and construction of new schools—whether local, magnet, or regional.

School districts, of course, know that they're going to be inundated by an influx of students, and preparing for enrollment increases does typically play a role in school construction planning today. Decisions about cafeteria and media center space, improvements in heating and ventilating systems, even siting considerations—all these are influenced by the coming increases in school populations.

In part because of these demographic pressures, therefore, we are already deep into a period when communities across the country are planning, designing, and building new high school space at an astonishing pace. At some point, perhaps a decade hence, this activity will significantly level off. The present time therefore represents *the* moment to focus on *the complete range of future needs,* since the many school facilities being planned and built right now will serve their communities for several generations. It's an opportunity that should not be wasted, for it's not likely to come again for a very long time.

POSSIBILITIES VERSUS REALITIES

The situation outlined above is not quite a stalemate. Change is occurring, though in fits and starts. To gain a better, more detailed understanding of how this situation looks *on the ground,* where decisions impacting the character of future schools are actually being made—and to see how educational leaders are dealing with the conflicting impulses to encourage and to resist change—Fletcher Thompson in 1999 and 2000 engaged in a statewide survey of Connecticut school district superintendents. The results were, in a word, mixed: the superintendents we surveyed seemed, as a whole, to be eager to institute some changes but doubtful about the value or feasibility of others.

During this same period, we also conducted extensive interviews with members of the Fletcher Thompson Educational Studio staff—architectural designers and project managers who, collectively, had worked on nearly 20 high school projects—asking them about the trends they were witnessing in high school design. The findings of both of these research efforts are combined and summarized below, and they provide a compelling look both at the possibilities for change and at the realities that impede change as these exist today. In what follows, we look first at a number of issues affecting curriculum, then go on to examine other technology issues, specific program areas, and, finally, a number of issues concerning the facility as a whole.

ISSUES AFFECTING CURRICULUM

Scheduling. Daily schedules at Connecticut high schools vary from fixed to rotating, with several block-scheduling variations. The eight-period day is standard, although some variations, utilized mostly for fiscal reasons, do exist. Truly modular schedules, which vary by day or by week, are still considered by superintendents to be too confusing, complicated, and/or expensive to administer. It goes without saying that resistance to the very idea of modular scheduling impedes the adoption of programs of study that are truly individualized.

Individualized Instruction. In general, teachers favor individualized instruction, but their efforts to introduce more individualized learning programs are stymied by lack of Internet access, lack of distance-learning availability, and a simple lack of time to make assignments and to follow up on students' progress.

Some savvy educators are teaming with application service providers (ASPs) to enable students to use low-cost, so-called "thin-clad" computers to access the Web only. These ASPs provide a wide array of curriculum-related information that allows teachers to individualize instruction efficiently. (Interestingly, school districts that just a few years ago were refusing donations from business of out-of-date computers are now once more welcoming such gifts, which, despite their relatively low processing speed and capacity, can be put to good use in Web access.)

Student Profiles, Data Warehousing, and Data Mining. Central to the solution of all curriculum development problems is each district's ability to access and manage information. Supported by computers, local area networks, and related peripheral equipment, some districts today are developing comprehensive student profiles with an eye toward improving counseling and remediation and providing an upgrade of basic academic skills as measured by the various standardized tests. (Such profiles can also be used to identify those students who may do harm to themselves or others.)

In some districts, data warehousing and data mining systems are allowing teachers to access the kind of student information that's necessary for writing educational "prescriptions." This data review is particularly helpful in gauging student strengths and weaknesses as the teacher and student prepare for testing and the school prepares for scheduling individualized programs of study.

Distance Learning. Although greatly desired, distance learning has not been widely or effectively implemented in Connecticut high schools because of a major practical barrier—the differences in schedules and calendars from one district to another. These differences make it extremely difficult to implement synchronous, "real time," instruction. Indeed, it is hard to find even two school districts that have the same class time slots.

Like some other states, Connecticut is currently installing a statewide fiber backbone—accessible by all K-12 schools, libraries, and colleges/universities—which will increase the speed and popularity of distance learning.

OTHER TECHNOLOGY ISSUES AND CONCERNS

Superintendents surveyed by Fletcher Thompson reported a host of desires relating to other technological systems—as well as a variety of problems with the systems they currently use. They also noted areas in which there has been some resistance to the introduction of new technologies.

In general, superintendents desired a smaller ratio of computers to students, with an emphasis on adding space and hardware for technology labs. They reported an increasing use of LAN/WAN network configurations, and the desire for greater speed—through the use of fiber optic cable and/or T-1 access—was universal. Some mentioned the desirability of wireless, especially in settings such as labs, where the mobility conferred by wireless laptops would be very advantageous.

High schools also reported increasing use of television for general communication and for special instructional purposes (such as a live coverage of a rocket blast-off).

High schools in general reported problems with network and (especially) website development and with related management and maintenance issues. Superintendents, who rely on consultants to design and install systems, typically complained that their systems do not function properly.

Though the superintendents we surveyed acknowledged the importance of acquiring and utilizing technology for the improvement of instruction, and though they consistently referenced the coming "dot-com curriculum," they felt that more leadership should be forthcoming in this area from the State Department of Education and from Connecticut's Regional Education centers. Many superintendents felt hard pressed to keep up with technological change and admitted to being consistently behind the learning curve. They also complained that it was hard to hire staff who are knowledgeable about the field and who are willing to stay in employment for a reasonable length of time.

In general, the introduction of voicemail has been welcomed, but there have been some instances of resistance by faculty who worry that voicemail increases their workload and, also, that it can delay face-to-face parent/teacher access.

Finally, intercom reliability and audibility continue to be major problems for many high schools, as do access, security, and control issues.

PROGRAM AREAS

Media Centers. New communications technologies are certain to have a very significant impact on the design of media centers in future high schools, but this is one area in which resistance to change is also very great. For example, the widespread adoption of electronic books and the electronic readers used to download and access them will make it possible to reduce the number of book stacks and the space that is now used to house them.

Such a thought, however, brings shivers to many librarians—a fear that's akin to that experienced by "tree huggers" in the face of the proverbial chainsaw. Eliminating some stacks is, however, inevitable and will probably start in the reference department. (The superintendents surveyed acknowledged the advent of the electronic reader but predicted that full-scale adoption would be a slow, evolutionary process.)

Despite resistance to this change, we believe it is safe to predict an eventual 50 percent cutback in stack space. As stack space wanes, the number of individual study stations and collaborative conferencing and teleconferencing rooms in media centers will increase, and we think that about half of the space now given over to stacks will be required for new individual workstations and collaborative environments. The net square footage reduction in a typical media center could therefore be as much as 25 percent.

Like librarians and media specialists, educators in general and the public at large believe that the media center should be the focal point of a school—a large, well-lighted, air-conditioned, attractive, comfortable space. It is still hard for most people to conceive of the effect that technology, properly employed, may ultimately have on the design and function of media centers.

Science Labs. The ninth and tenth grade science lab is gradually evolving into a one-room, combined presentation and virtual lab space. At those grade levels (at least in some schools), experiments are now being conducted virtually on computer screens, eliminating the need for glassware, special furniture, and lab-counter gas, water, and power sources. It is much easier and more efficient to perform dissections using a popular anatomy software like "ADAM" than on a real animal! These all-purpose science labs for the lower grades do not need prep rooms or separate presentation classrooms. The superintendents we surveyed generally agreed that ninth/tenth grade science labs could be generic, technologically supported classrooms. (This change, by the way, would enable us to reduce a new high school's total science square footage by approximately 20 percent.)

Advanced-placement chemistry, biology, and physics courses will, however, continue to require labs in which students can perform real, hands-on experiments (perhaps supplemented by virtual guidance). Well-equipped labs—with gas, water, electricity, and associated code/safety items—will therefore remain essential necessities for advanced science courses.

Physical Education. Unfortunately, we have not found ways in which technology will allow us to condense physical education space and/or schedules. In fact, one could easily make the argument that the future high school's physical education components should be *increased* in size. It is possible, however, that with sophisticated scheduling, the use of improved artificial turf, and the application of the inflatable roof and/or multi-purpose fieldhouse/superdome structure, phys ed facilities can be designed and built to accommodate multiple uses in a weatherproof and more cost-effective environment.

It may also be possible to individualize physical education instruction by giving credit for out-of-school activities such as participation on a soccer team or following an exercise program at home. Clearly, physical education can be acquired after or before regular school hours, but any facility savings achieved by such scheduling would probably be offset by increased facility demand by a wide variety of groups.

Superintendents in our survey generally agreed that demands on athletic space are growing inexorably and that careful scheduling—with an eye toward both maintenance and use—could increase efficiency. Some superintendents also appeared open to the fieldhouse solution: one superintendent was successfully using a fieldhouse, and another was in the process of building a fieldhouse. (Both these projects were renovations.) The cost-saving fieldhouse solution makes a great deal of sense in temperate climates like Connecticut's.

Fine Arts and Auditorium. Like phys ed, the arts are likely to require more, not less, space in the future high school. Student involvement in the arts is growing, and the performing arts are viewed as increasingly important, both for the school population and for the wider community. Practice room and rehearsal space as well as space to store instruments and house audio/visual equipment are showing up in more and more building specifications. (Spaces for live practice and performance seem to serve as an antidote to the anonymity associated with Internet interaction and virtual "experience.")

Communities are asking for high school auditoriums with large seating capacities so that everyone can gather to appreciate, celebrate, and debate. While a square footage cutback is hard to recommend here, combined town/school use can make more efficient use of fine arts and auditorium space. In general, superintendents in our survey desired auditoriums that had the capacity to seat the entire student body at one time, but they admitted that it can be extremely difficult to sell taxpayers on the nonreimbursable cost of such facilities.

Practical Arts (Industrial Arts, Unified Arts, and/or Technology). As in some parts of the science curriculum, some instruction in the practical arts lends itself to computer-based instruction and the virtual-experience mode of learning. But hands-on experience remains a necessity. One has to assume that to be able to saw, drill, and use a tape measure will always be important. To fix a leaky faucet, wire a plug, and change a flat tire are skills that will also be with us for quite a while. Once again, it is hard to envision square footage reductions in practical arts; in fact, more space may be needed as computer repair training at the high school level becomes more and more commonplace.

Superintendents participating in our survey noted the demise of enrollment in what used to be called industrial arts. They also noted sharp declines in the purchase of expensive equipment and supplies for this type of instruction. Simultaneously, though, they cited the increasing need for education in how to repair computers and install high-tech infrastructure. In general, they felt that some reduction in practical arts space would be beneficial, and, in fact, several superintendents reported that they were in the process of eliminating all "shops," with the exception of those that are computer-related.

Specialized Programs. Many schools are expressing interest in adding classrooms equipped for instruction in childcare, health, TV production, and aquaculture/agriculture.

Districts that focus on "college prep" academics have less interest in specialty programs—as is evidenced by the phase-out of industrial arts instruction in their schools. On the other hand, districts with relatively low college entrance rates are enthusiastic about adding more specialty courses. Superintendents' attitudes about specialty programs are, as one might imagine, all over the map: One superintendent responding to our survey wanted a class in jewelry making, while another scoffed at the idea. If it is possible to discern a trend here, it seems to be away from offering specialty courses—but only very slightly.

Alternative schools—educational facilities designed to house those members of the high school population who have behavior problems or for other reasons seem to need a separate environment—appear to be growing in number. But most new high schools do not incorporate on-site alternative schools. (Rather, these students, who account for 3 to 8 percent of the total high school-age population, are generally housed in separate locations.)

FACILITY ISSUES

Conferencing Space. It is a rare high school today that has adequate administration space. Because conferencing is at the very heart of the administrative process, enough space should be available that administrators, counselors, nurses, recruiters, planning and placement teams (PPTs), students, parents, and visiting officials can do their work efficiently, collaboratively, and well. Such space should be equipped with teleconferencing capability. The average 20-year-old high school probably needs to increase its administrative square footage by about 20 percent.

As the teacher becomes more of a counselor, the need for the traditional sort of interaction between students and counselors diminishes—*but* that will be offset by an increasing need for one-on-one interaction between students and their teacher/counselors. The traditional counselor will spend more time training the teacher to counsel the student.

With the advent of counseling related to students' genetic capacities and the dispensing of designer drugs, the nurse's office will, we think, expand into a nurse/doctor space with room for conferencing and probably for drug prescribing and distributing.

The superintendents we polled agreed that increases are needed in the space allocated for nurses, counselors, and administrators. They also stressed the need for more conference room.

Students, of course, need conferencing space, too. If a school has conflict resolution, anger mitigation, or personal problem-solving programs, conferencing space must be allocated for these purposes. And the movement to help young people learn about and use democratic principles through collaborative learning is likewise influencing high schools' architectural requirements. The higher-order thinking program called "HOT"—a good example of a democratic learning program—calls for large spaces for assembly and smaller conferencing and communication opportunities. (This program is usually supported by sophisticated electronic communication systems.) And student government organizations also need space that allows for large group discussion and voting.

Food Service. Most high schools continue to operate their own in-house kitchens, though there has been some movement toward outside vendors taking over high school food service operations. The real quandary facing most schools, however, involves being able to move large numbers of students in and out of the cafeteria rapidly while at the same time offering students a wide-ranging menu. To this end, automated credit, inventory, and bookkeeping systems are being successfully utilized. (Garbage control systems are also of great importance.)

Security, Health, and Accessibility. Superintendents participating in our survey cited security and air quality as the top facility-related problems. Understanding and meeting code requirements of all kinds, especially disabled-access mandates, is also a great concern. Wheelchair access, safety rails on bleachers, and the installation of Braille signage are examples of the multitude of disabled-access mandates now influencing high school design.

New high schools today are generally being equipped with a variety of security systems and devices, including ID entrance verification, surveillance cameras, portable communication systems, protection alarms, and space for security personnel. The focus is on observing and controlling the movement of the student body, and this adds to the need for efficient traffic-flow patterns discussed above. (Part of the popularity of the "loop"-style circulation pattern chosen by so many schools today has to do with its ability to impose an efficient traffic pattern and accommodate maximum traffic comfortably.)

Over-sensitive fire alarm systems that become dirty, go off frequently, and require extensive maintenance are a common nuisance. Air handling systems that are not well balanced and that include a maze of ducts (which gather dirt and are accused of being germ breeders) are matters of concern during the portion of the year when the building must be heated, particularly the fall and spring "swing" seasons.

In most high schools today, air conditioning is limited to central office spaces and computer labs, but, as education becomes year-round, the air conditioning of the entire building becomes more necessary for health as well as comfort reasons. Allergy-related sickness—and complaints and demands by worried parents—are on the increase. Special machinery to clean air in classrooms with special-needs children is now being mandated.

Automatic building controls for heating, ventilating, and air conditioning are desired—they can save a school a lot of money—but also feared, since they can pose problems when they do not work properly.

The "Large School Versus Small School" Debate. Many have argued that students are more likely to be lonely and lost in a large school than in a small one. Though the superintendents we polled for the most part favored smaller high schools—in the 1,000- to 1,200-student range—the preference for smaller schools no longer makes as much sense as it once did. The traditional barriers to communication imposed by walls, distance, and size are becoming progressively less important. The existence of an "intranet community" in each new school will allow students to meet and get to know one another online through a variety of interactive modes.

As communications technologies support interactivity no matter what the size of the school, economics becomes more important as a deciding factor. Large high schools are able to provide a wider variety of program choices because of economies of scale, and, on a per-student basis, they are cheaper to build. A high school for 3,000 students has less square footage than two 1,500-student high schools. And, of course, large high schools can be broken down into "houses," which give students a greater sense of belonging. Therefore, despite continuing resistance to the idea, the large high school seems to make sense for the future.

SUPERINTENDENT/ARCHITECT COLLABORATION IS KEY

Solutions to many of the problems mentioned in this chapter are well understood, both by architects and by school superintendents. Unfortunately, there is often little communication between the architect and the superintendent beyond developing and presenting building specifications for board of education approval. The matter is then typically turned over to a building committee, and few superintendents have the time to attend the numerous building committee meetings, choosing instead to delegate the responsibility or to decline the opportunity altogether. As a result, solutions—which require conviction and foresight to formulate and significant leadership to implement—fall by the wayside. And, even where solutions do emerge, gaining approval from taxpayers, who tend to be conservative, can be a difficult job—but one that is made easier with the superintendent's participation.

The proliferation of new communications technologies—and their increasing affordability—puts us at the crossroads of change. By working together, we can make a difference. As we explore over the next four chapters of this book, collaboration is the key to effective planning and design of today's high schools—so that they can meet future challenges.

Part II: Creating Schools Collaboratively

Chapter 3

The Process of Creation— In Need of Improvement

In this book's Introduction, we stressed the importance of collaborative problem-solving as an essential element in the new philosophy of education now transforming high school curricula across the country. We emphasized, too, that helping high school students to develop the skill of working together to find solutions is vital to maintaining our society's democracy and improving our democratic institutions.

Tellingly, collaboration is just as important in the planning and design of new high school buildings that will successfully meet future challenges. Too often, though, collaboration gets short-circuited. The creation of a new building—or an addition to or renovation of an existing facility—involves a large expenditure of funds and relies on a tradition-bound set of procedures that can get in the way of "forward-looking," "outside-the-box" creativity and innovation. Checks and balances incorporated into the process are aimed primarily at containing cost and often provide little room for educational or architectural vision.

In this chapter, we closely examine the typical process of creating a new high school in Connecticut, commenting on its inherent flaws and suggesting ways in which it could be improved. Although the process outlined here is in some ways particular to Connecticut, in its main features it does not differ greatly from the way in which a new public high school is created almost anywhere in the country. The major steps in any such process are these:

- Getting the idea off the ground

- Developing an educational specification (perhaps with a consultant's assistance)

- Earning approval from the state department of education and the state legislature

- Hiring an architect

- Gaining passage of a referendum, followed by the design and construction process itself

In reviewing this process—with an eye toward discovering how it could work better—two things must be kept especially in mind:

- *The educational specification plays a crucially important role in a project's success.* A good "ed spec" pays heed to the interests of all the "stakeholders" in the process. It incorporates the community's vision of the future. It gives the architect sufficient guidance to design a facility that will truly meet present and future educational needs. And, if it is well written and used effectively, the educational specification can be a primary tool in convincing local voters to pass a school-building referendum. (For more on educational specifications—and a collaborative process for their development—see Chapter 4.)

- *Democratic collaboration—and a process that fosters collaboration—requires leadership at all levels:* from parents, faculty, school
  principals and other administrators, superintendents, local government
  leaders, state boards of education, and state legislators. Improving the
  process by which new high schools come into being may involve
  making some fundamental changes in the way the process works—
  altering the time-honored formulas that can stultify innovation and
  vision. Changing entrenched patterns requires an adventurous spirit
  and some risk-taking, and we challenge all participants to envision, and
  to experiment with, ways of making both the process and the product
  better. Beyond this, an improved process will require one "point
  person" to ensure continuity throughout the life of the project, from the
  inception of the idea through the completion of construction. We
  believe that this role falls most naturally to the district superintendent.

INCEPTION

Let's begin our look at the process from the moment that a new facility is
first thought of. It's easy to imagine the kick-off conversation, which usually
occurs in an administrator's office—most likely the district superintendent's,
but sometimes that of a school principal. The issue driving the conversation
is sometimes a problematic, antiquated existing facility, but it's more likely
that expanding enrollment or a programmatic space need is what precipitates
the interchange.

The conversation between superintendent and principal might go something like this: The principal speaks of how desperately a new facility is
needed, and the superintendent responds,

"Joe, I know we need it, but this is an election year" or

*"Joe, we sure need it but I'm about ready to put a budget on the table and
I don't want to raise more eyebrows,"* or

*"Joe, I know we need it, but last year the town council asked us to hold off
on capital projects."*

At about the same time that this kick-off conversation is happening, the
Parent/Teacher Association is also starting to focus on the problem,
claiming, "We've got to put our kids first. We can afford a new building, and
we shouldn't wait any longer."

Then, an aspiring politician—maybe a town council–type with young
children—will start beating the drum. The dawning possibility of creating a
new school gets debated in round after round of backroom conversations,
as community leader after community leader joins the discussion and starts
to probe—perhaps even visiting the existing school and pursuing a
"What's the real scoop?" mode of investigation.

[Comment: The local political process, for the most part, pays little attention to enrollment projections and need statements prepared by educators. Generally, municipal leaders wait until classrooms—or pipes!—are bursting before even considering a major facility expenditure. They do not, in general, trust educators, feeling that the best way to keep expenditures—both operating and capital—down is to squeeze the system until undeniable evidence of underfunding presents itself. This backwards philosophy is pervasive throughout the facility creation process. For instance, it sometimes seems as if beating up on the educator, architect, or contractor and getting them to "sharpen their pencils" is far more important than meeting students' needs in a timely fashion or taking steps to ensure a quality design that is truly visionary.]

THE EDUCATIONAL SPECIFICATION

The description of the project is usually called the *educational specification*—"ed spec," for short. Some ed specs are highly developed and detailed documents (running from 20 to 30 pages) that give clear direction; others are a page long and require an interpretation process that entails significant discussion and a great deal of imagination.

[Comment: School districts need more guidance on how to write a good, useful education specification, which we attempt to do in the following chapter, "Collaboration in the Development of Educational Specifications." It would also be a good idea for the state departments of education to give a detailed definition of what is expected in a specification—some do, some don't—and to require such documentation as part of the school construction approval application document. A review by state department of education architectural consultants of the specification and development procedure might well provide for a more cost-effective and efficient building process.]

STATE APPROVAL PROCESS

In Connecticut, the State Department of Education requires a project application one year in advance of state legislative approval of a facility. The infamous ED-049 facility application form—generally thought of as a "placeholder"—must be approved by both the local board of education and the municipal legislative body prior to submission. The 049 form asks the superintendent of schools to identify the problem and to obtain an estimate of the cost of correcting it. Further, the form asks the local district to estimate state reimbursement in accordance with a funding formula based on the town's or city's socioeconomic need and adjusted for the size of the student body and whether the project involves an elementary, middle, or high school.

A town will usually bring an architect on board to help in preparing the 049 form. At this stage, architects often offer their services on a noncontractual basis, hoping to develop a relationship with the district with the aim of getting a contract for the project once the approval process has been completed. The architect treads a fine line in developing project costs—keeping one eye on the salability of the bottom-line figure, the other on how well the educational specification will be met. Having to return to the State Department of Education for additional funds after initial approval is not desirable.

In almost all cases, state reimbursement does not cover *all* components of a project: for example, the state might refuse to reimburse part of a project on the grounds that that portion of the building (e.g., a portion of the auditorium) is not "educational" or that planned space is more lavish than what is necessary to meet basic needs. Just how far above state reimbursement levels a project can go is always an interesting question. Decisions to include nonreimbursable components are usually based on an analysis of state reimbursements and on the town's desire and ability to support education beyond that level. It's not uncommon for a wealthier town to decide to build a more expensive and lavish facility because its citizens want "the best" for their children (and, of course, because the town can afford to do so).

The state education commissioner may waive reimbursement requirements for good and sufficient reason—and, in fact, the commissioner regularly does waive them for magnet schools designed to regionalize and integrate functions, as well as for urban schools that need a wide variety of special spaces relating, for example, to bilingual education, the orientation of students who are recent immigrants, special education, and/or behavior/ security problems.

Submission of the 049 form is routinely put off until the last minute—June 30 (that is, the end of the fiscal year)—because town bodies rarely act unless faced with a deadline. Local officials voting to approve submission of the form are usually persuaded by arguments that the submission is only a "placeholder" and that holding off on approval will postpone the decision for at least a year, which might prove costly. Those who vote against approving the submission, however, know that their own act of approval—and the approval of the state board of education and legislature that will follow—in fact represent the actual beginning of the project.

[Comment: The placeholder nature of the 049 application and, in many districts, the lack of available funding to hire an architect to develop and review educational specifications before submission tend to produce a relatively casual, incomplete, and poorly thought-out "first look" at the facility problem. Availability of state-reimbursed preliminary feasibility study funding would allow for a more thorough startup process and would

produce 049 documents that more accurately represent what the facilities that are ultimately built will actually be like.]

The state legislature's approval of the project is usually routine and based on the State Department of Education's recommendations. Legislators often talk of capping the amount of money to be authorized. They also talk of revising state standards and funding formulas. Historically, however, no action has been taken—other than to put local legislators and superintendents on notice that delaying submission of a project might mean having to face revised legislation in a subsequent year.

[Comment: Legislators spend most of their time worrying about levels of expenditure—and very little time reviewing and second-guessing the state approval process or looking at the actual projects. Under its own time pressure, the State Department of Education has little time during the approvals process to examine educational specifications, choosing instead to focus on enrollment validation and on questions of what will and will not be reimbursed. The state department could help the process by providing a database of existing project statistics that would be useful to architects, educators, boards of education, and building committees. For instance, comparative square footage data is not presently available on either a state or a national basis. Such a database could outline exemplary educational specifications. One district, for instance, could look at the science lab or media center solution achieved by another district (in the state or somewhere else in the country).]

THE BUILDING COMMITTEE

After the 049 form is approved, the town leadership usually passes the project on to a building committee (sometimes, a town council will itself serve as the building committee). Some towns have permanent building committees. Others appoint committees to work on specific projects. Occasionally, a committee includes representation from the local board of education, but more routinely the committee is made up of local contractors, lawyers, architects, and educational advocates. In many cases the local taxpayer association is represented. (In an ideal situation, all these constituencies would be represented.)

The building committee usually relies on board of education approval of the specification or concept when accepting the project and routinely explains its charge as building "to the spec"—*not* identifying and/or interpreting educational needs.

THE ARCHITECT

Before engaging an architect, the building committee, with assistance from an administrative clerk of the town, issues a request for proposal (RFP) in accordance with state and local laws regarding bidding and hiring. Hiring a professional architect does not require accepting a low bid, but the price of service is almost always a central consideration in making a selection.

[Comment: As an alternative to a bottom-line based selection process, the qualifications-based selection (QBS) process should be considered.]

The architect responds to the RFP with a booklet submission describing the firm, including bios of the team that will work on the project, and outlining why the firm is suited for the job. Based on its review of the submissions it receives, the building committee selects four or five architectural firms to "short list" and schedules interviews with these firms. The architectural firm designates a team—typically consisting of a principal of the firm, a project architect, a designer, an engineer, a landscape specialist, and perhaps other participants—to attend the interview, which usually lasts from half an hour to an hour.

During the consideration process, the building committee may check firms' references, visit facilities (completed or under construction) designed by the short-listed firms, and sometimes visit the architects' offices.

[Comment: Unfortunately, most superintendents of schools elect not *to be involved in this part of the process—and, in fact, don't even bother to designate someone from the superintendent's office to participate in building committee meetings. This is a real mistake, since the superintendent—or his or her designee—can be the "glue" that holds together the goals of the board of education, the town, and the building committee.]*

THE REFERENDUM

Most towns are required by local charter to have a public vote, or referendum, approving the particular project. Needless to say, voters will want as much information as possible before offering up their "yea" or "nay."

Unfortunately, in most cases voters have trouble getting the information they need in order to decide whether the expenditure is wise and whether the projected facility will really meet students' needs. Voters who go to the building committee seeking information will most likely encounter what amounts to "buck-passing." Most building committees don't want to spend money developing information on an unapproved project, so they turn the matter over to the architect. But most architects are unwilling to do extensive design work on an unapproved project, which may be voted down, and so the architect refers to the specification, which was created by the superintendent of schools and approved by the board of education and the town legislative body to facilitate the filling-out of the infamous 049 form—and which is therefore likely to be an inadequate description of the project!

[Comment: In the referendum environment, facility-development rationales are usually based on enrollment needs, the age of an existing facility, and affordability concerns—not on educational or programmatic issues. (Unsurprisingly, referendum issues tend to revolve around how much the property tax rate will increase if the facility is approved.) It doesn't have to be this way. The educational specification, if it were written well and clearly stated programmatic needs, could serve as the centerpiece of a referendum-approval rationale.

We cannot overemphasize the importance of the superintendent's leadership during the referendum phase. Unfortunately, exercising such leadership requires a great deal of time—which may be in very short supply—and it can be politically dangerous. It's more than likely that the superintendent, not having the time to spend and concerned about political ramifications, will simply stand aside. In this leadership vacuum, the simple logic of dollars and cents may take over—and the need to improve educational programs may get lost.

Of course, a quality architect will attempt to provide the needed leadership, but, absent strong support from the superintendent, the architect will lack the local knowledge and the clout to speak on behalf of the program. Good architects do their best to meet specification needs and provide a quality product, but they're mostly forced to bend to the wind when cost issues prevail.]

CONCLUSION

As we've seen, the process by which new educational facilities are currently created in Connecticut (and, by extension, in much of the rest of the country, as well) is a seriously flawed one. Responsibility is passed from authority to authority. Educational specifications are often poorly developed. As a result, students' needs and educational vision are given short shrift. But, as we hope we've also conveyed, the process can be greatly improved.

For starters, the State Department of Education could be of enormous help if it were to provide comparative (state and national) square footage data, if it were to require submission of a detailed educational specification in the initial approval process, and if it were to review that specification thoroughly before making a recommendation to the legislature. (Legislators, too, would do well to concern themselves at least as much with educational vision as they do with expenditures.)

Ideally, the development of an ed spec should be a highly collaborative process involving all the stakeholders in the community. Often, the architect is asked to do more than design and oversee construction of a facility.

Involvement of the architect in the development of an educational specification is common. This isn't necessarily a bad thing, but having the architect develop and market educational specifications *without* appropriate support from the educational staff and other stakeholders can be counterproductive.

As it stands today, the process of facility creation tends to limit educational vision, architectural creativity, and the community's ability to meet student needs. Given the prevailing bottom-line orientation, it is ironic that flaws inherent in the existing process may actually wind up costing the taxpayer more rather than less, as poorly envisioned schools demonstrate their inadequacy over time.

Chapter 4

Collaboration in the Development of Educational Specifications

A first-rate, useful educational specification ("ed spec") does four things:

- *It describes the vision* motivating the creation of the new facility (or renovation or addition) and its place in the wider community, incorporating the perspectives of all of the facility's stakeholders.

- *It provides an objective, quantifiable rationale* for the new facility, drawing on and citing demographic information about anticipated enrollments and the character of the student body over the coming years.

- *It presents a detailed, thorough list of programmatic requirements and of the spaces that will be needed to implement the program,* paying close attention to the school's programmatic needs and operational capabilities.

- *It generates excitement and enthusiasm for the new facility throughout the community.*

Although the ed spec ultimately functions as *the* primary resource used by the architect in designing the building, it is vitally important to remember that the educational specification is an *educational,* not an architectural, document. Some districts produce ed specs that are too vague—specs that fail to identify program needs and related projected enrollments. But some school districts go too far, wasting time by suggesting design approaches that may not be used or construction items that may not be needed in the creation of the actual facility.

There is no single method for producing a good, useful ed spec: different districts take different approaches, any of which might be successful. Some districts rely on the superintendent of schools to write the educational specification, and, if the superintendent devotes energy to the task, is a good writer, and is diligent in seeking others' input, this method may produce a superior ed spec. Many districts, however, hire consultants to guide them through this sometimes challenging process. Some architectural firms offer such consulting services, and, in an important sense, an architect is a natural choice, since many architectural firms can draw on a wealth of historical data and technical resources and because it is an architect who will ultimately have to use the specification to develop drawings. But, no matter who is providing the consulting service, that firm will have to turn to the educational staff and other stakeholders for information.

In fact, although any of these approaches might work well, the one rule that *any* ed-spec development process should follow is *to invite the early and ongoing involvement of all of the new facility's stakeholders.* And there is no getting around the fact that soliciting their participation—and thereby generating their enthusiasm—is a lengthy and complex process that, to succeed, must be carefully managed. As we stress again and again in this book, democracy takes time and requires skilled leadership.

STEP 1: THE VISION

Don't make the mistake of dismissing the *vision* that guides the creation of a new facility as "the soft stuff." The facts and figures come later, but articulating a comprehensive vision of educational philosophy and of the facility's role in the life of the wider community is *the absolutely essential first step in producing a successful ed spec.* Drafting a vision statement helps the community to see where it is headed, to organize its priorities, to investigate new approaches to education and curriculum design (and to decide which of these will best serve its children), and —at its very best—to boldly address the challenges that the community believes the future will bring. In a sense, everything else—from the number of science labs, to the size of the gymnasium, to the openness of the school to the wider community of users—follows from the vision guiding the building's planning, design, and construction.

The best vision statements—we provide an excellent example at the end of Chapter 6—are extremely thorough, addressing virtually every aspect of the curriculum and the building's non-education-related functions *but stopping short* of specifying the numbers and kinds of spaces necessary to implement the vision. The vision statement gives the community the opportunity to be ambitious, hopeful, forward-looking—in a word, *visionary.* This is not to say that the vision should be unrealistic—and, in fact, a certain amount of realism regarding budgetary and operational issues will naturally be imposed by the collaborative process by which the vision statement comes into being.

Although the language of the statement itself is likely to be drafted by a small group of people or even by a single individual (perhaps the superintendent), it should represent the work and collective thinking of the entire community. Gathering that knowledge is best accomplished through a series of conversations and meetings with the various constituencies—students, principal and administrative staff, faculty, other school staff, taxpayers and community groups, and so on. There's no hard-and-fast requirement regarding the format of such conversations and meetings: some might be set up as "town hall"–type hearings that the entire community is invited to attend, others might be intensive focus groups with limited numbers of staff or parents, others might be one-on-one conversations between the superintendent and academic department heads. Consultants generally come equipped with strategies for gathering this input effectively, but it's clear that such methods should be tailored to the needs of the specific community and school and the working styles of superintendent, principal, and faculty. What's also clear is that—for the entire community's wishes, needs, desires, and insights to be genuinely represented in the final vision statement—dozens of separate meetings may be entailed.

There's no easy way to categorize (or limit) the kinds of questions that might be considered during such exchanges, except to say that they should be somewhat broad and general in scope. Here are just a few examples:

- What are our projected enrollments for five, ten, and fifteen years from now? Are the community's demographics changing, and how? Should we anticipate a greater (or lesser) need for ESL programs, for example, or cultural orientation programs for recent-immigrant students? Is the demand for special education-related components likely to grow more intense in the coming years?

- How much emphasis do we want to place on work- or career-oriented programs? And what kinds of career-oriented programs do we want the school to specialize in? (Traditional practical arts? Computer programming, wiring, and maintenance?)

- How are changes in state graduation requirements likely to affect our program?

- How are college requirements likely to change?

- How should the school be organized? For example, if the new facility is a high school, will it be organized as a large single school or divided into a number of "houses"?

- How will the wider community use the building? Will it be a place where town meetings will be held? Will the media center be open to the general public during certain hours? Will community arts groups be using the auditorium or other spaces? (And so on.)

STEP 2: THE PROGRAM

Once the vision statement has been prepared, it's time to begin translating the broad agenda that it lays out into the specifics of spaces, the numbers of students (and other facility users) who will occupy them, and the key relationships among spaces that will best achieve the vision statement's curricular and other programmatic goals. (By "key relationships," we mean things like adjacencies: for example, should the media center be contiguous to the main lobby in order to facilitate use by the wider community?)

Of course, the superintendent or ed spec consultant (perhaps working hand in hand with a "vision committee") will already have begun to gather some of this kind of information: it's inevitable that the vision of the new school facility will have been shaped by an awareness of the character and size of the student body, for example, or by operational issues regarding the availability of faculty who could teach certain kinds of courses, etc. But, until now, the process should have steered clear of developing specific programmatic solutions.

The key to devising these programmatic solutions successfully is—once again—*collaborative process*. The principle motivating a collaborative approach is a simple one: the stakeholders in any given curricular or extracurricular area are not just the people who have the greatest investment in that area, they're also the people who have the greatest *knowledge* about what it will take to implement the vision statement's agenda in that area. This is best demonstrated by example:

Suppose the vision statement, in a section on physical education, has spoken in broad terms of the need to give equal attention and programmatic weight to both girls' and boys' sports. Translating this overarching agenda into space (and related) needs will require that those responsible for developing the programmatic portion of the ed spec consult with physical education faculty and coaches to determine (for example):

- The number and types of indoor spaces (gyms, a fieldhouse, gymnastics rooms, weight-training rooms, pools, etc.) necessary to accomplish the program, and what each space will be used for. (The size and makeup of the student body, state phys ed requirements, and the numbers of students likely to take advantage of sports programs are among the determinants, here.)

- The number and types of outdoor spaces (playing fields, track and field facilities, etc.) required, and what each space will be used for.

- Locker and equipment-storage space requirements.

- Training rooms, coaching space, and video rooms.

- Office space requirements.

During this phase of the ed spec's development, the vision statement should guide the approach to the "operational realities." But efficient use of the *entire* physical plant should be a goal, since no community will want to pay for an overdesigned facility (a "Taj Mahal").

Once a complete list of required/desired spaces and a description of the population(s) that will use those spaces have been compiled, it's better to stop and wait for the architect to assign rough square footages to the spaces. If the person or committee developing the ed spec (without an architect's assistance, that is) goes ahead and assigns square footage numbers to the list of spaces, it's quite likely that the architect hired to design the building will have to revisit the matter, meeting with all the people involved in order to test the assumptions they used to determine size. (In plain terms, it's probably a waste of time for anyone but an architect to assign square footage numbers to the project's components.)

Despite the fact that any new high school building will be "customized" to meet a given community's specific educational needs and vision, those charged with the development of an educational specification may find it very helpful to have some sort of model to work from, or to play their own ideas off against. Later in this book, we provide just such a model—a somewhat generic, though comprehensive, high school ed spec based on forward-looking work done by one Connecticut community. (See Chapter 8.)

FROM THE ABSTRACT TO THE CONCRETE

Once the programmatic details of the ed spec have been developed, it's time to begin assigning "numbers" to the project—first, square footages; then, dollar estimates of the cost of the facility as outlined in the spec. If the district has retained an architect to help develop the ed spec, this stage represents a continuation of the process; if not, this is the moment when an architect must be brought on board to begin translating the desires embodied in the ed spec into the actualities of size and budget.

It may be somewhat surprising to those unfamiliar with the process, but, once the architect has been given a list of desired spaces and probable occupancies, it's a fairly routine matter to determine the probable square footages of each of those spaces and, in turn, the probable gross and net square footages of the entire facility. (The "net" consists of all the space that will be used for programmatic purposes; the "gross" includes all the other space—corridor space, infrastructure space, and so on—that will be needed to make the facility function.) An experienced architect will draw on a wealth of historical data to make these determinations.

From there, it is again a fairly routine matter to come up with a ballpark cost for the building. Here, it's a matter of applying historical data *plus* comprehensive knowledge of the construction market in a given area or region, and any good estimator—whether the estimator is part of the architect's team, or a construction manager, or an independent estimating firm—will be able, once the square footages have been calculated, to apply the necessary formulas and to work out a fairly accurate construction budget, both for the entire facility and for each of its major components. These numbers won't be perfectly precise, of course. (Estimates will become much more accurate after design has been performed, when estimators will be able to calculate amounts of building materials needed, labor time for specific trades, and so on.) But these "rough" numbers will be good enough to guide further decision-making.

What *further* decision-making? Well, experience shows that the specific programmatic desires articulated in an ed spec often outdistance the amount of money that a community can actually afford—or the amount that the voters are likely to approve in a referendum. It isn't until this point in the process—when the "rough" (though surprisingly accurate) construction cost estimates are in—that decision-makers can begin to adjust the ed spec's program to the financial realities that the community faces.

Undoubtedly, the community's governing body (e.g., the town council) will have begun this whole process with a certain overall budget in mind. If that figure is, say, $40 million and the rough estimate comes in at $60 million, then it's necessary to return to the ed spec and begin prioritizing, distinguishing between "needs" and "wants," culling less essential program elements, and looking for ways in which spaces can be put to multiple use—anything, in other words, that will reduce the amount of space and therefore the construction cost while maintaining as much of the desired program as possible.

This, too, is a collaborative process, and there's often some room for negotiation between the building committee or board of education and the community's political leadership. It may, in other words, be possible to salvage at least some of the elements that cause the envisioned facility to exceed the original budget limit. And it bears pointing out that this kind of negotiation is made all the easier *if* the process has been collaborative from the very beginning, since all the stakeholders—including those who hold the purse strings—will have been involved in envisioning the new school building and will want it to match as closely as possible all the accumulating expectations and hopes.

In fact, that's a *key* insight—and a good way to end this chapter before turning to collaboration during the design and project management stages. As we said earlier, one of the chief reasons to do the ed spec right is to *generate excitement and enthusiasm for the new facility throughout the community.* If all the stakeholders feel that they've participated in the ed spec's development—and if they all have some understanding of the new facility's potential benefits to the entire community—they'll be much more willing to go the extra mile to make the building as good as possible. When they've been an integral part of the process, town council members are more likely to understand the need for a particular program element and to increase the allowable budget accordingly. And voters will be much more likely to respond positively when the matter is put before them in a referendum. A good ed spec is good politics. *It builds community.*

Chapter 5

Collaborative Design and Project Management

Tomorrow's educational environments must accommodate new approaches to teaching and learning while serving the needs of all of a facility's "stakeholders"—that is, the members of the community who have an interest in the outcome of the project.

The U.S. Department of Education has identified six design principles for the planning and designing of schools that also serve as centers of the community. These principles have been endorsed by the American Institute of Architects (AIA), the Council for Educational Facilities Planners International (CEFPI), Urban Educational Facilities for the 21st Century (UEF), and the American Association of Retired Persons (AARP). The principles challenge architects to design learning environments that

- Enhance teaching and learning and accommodate the needs of all learners

- Serve as a center of the community

- Result from a planning/design process involving all stakeholders

- Provide for health, safety, and security

- Make effective use of all available resources

- Allow for flexibility and adaptability to changing needs

The architects and educators of Fletcher-Thompson, Inc., have developed architectural planning and design solutions that give concrete expression to these abstract concepts. We believe that our approach to school building planning and design can serve as a model for other educators, planners, and architects—and for communities across the country—as we enter the new millennium.

DESIGN APPROACH

Time and again, our extensive experience in the planning and design of school facilities has proved that the *process* by which a project is initiated is critical to its overall success. We have come to believe that a major factor contributing to a project's success is to organize the project properly from the very start. A well-organized project—led by an expertly staffed team—ensures that a district's educational goals of quality, cost, and schedule can be fulfilled.

The importance of continued community support over the life of a project cannot be overemphasized. Neither should we underestimate the pressures placed on municipal governments and local school districts with regard to costs and the performance of their facilities. Today, better-informed, better-educated voters are holding building committees and municipal and school officials accountable for both first-time costs and long-term performance of construction projects.

To *maximize project value* and to minimize maintenance and operating costs, important decisions regarding cost and overall quality must be made early in the design process and must be clearly communicated to all participants. The goal, here, is to minimize the need for changes late in the design process, when such changes are decidedly less effective and may compromise the project's quality or scope.

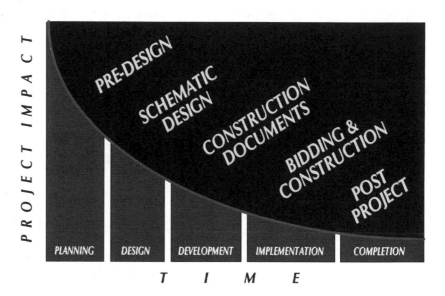

The creation of a new high school is a complex process involving the balancing of many variables. The following list of design-related issues, arranged by category, is not necessarily complete, but it does show the wide scope of issues that should be brought to the table from the very start of the design process. (Note that these are *general* issues, not specific educational/programmatic issues, which are discussed in detail in Chapter 8, "The High School of the Future: Design Requirements for Specific Curricular Areas.")

MISSION

- Define expectations

- Understand the difference between traditional and contemporary architecture

- Create a sense of cohesiveness

- Represent vision for the future

- Understand the role of the building in its community

COMMUNITY USE

- Welcome community to the campus

- Create well-defined entrances and internal pathways

- Integrate the needs of multiple users: students, parents, faculty, administrators, community groups, continuing education programs, etc.

- Provide appropriate levels of security, indoors and out, for both daytime and nighttime use

BUILDING CONTEXT AND MASSING

- Understand the site—its limitations and potential

- Understand site preparation/remediation issues

- Understand environmental issues

- Harmonize larger and smaller built elements, creating a variety of scales

- Integrate building and landscape

BUILDING MATERIALS

- Use local materials, whenever possible

- Provide a sense of place through the use of materials

- Develop a unifying and distinctive design vocabulary

- Emphasize interplay of texture, shade, shadow, color, and light

- Emphasize the interplay of natural and artificial lighting

- Understand the importance of accents

LANDSCAPING

- Configure building elements in a way that defines outdoor spaces
- Specify maintainable planting program

- Develop designs consistent with all standards for outdoor lighting and furnishings

- Provide flexibility for special events

- Understand the impact of landscaping decisions on security issues

ENTRANCE AND CIRCULATION

- Provide a variety of choices

- Provide multiple, adequately lighted entrances

- Understand the difference between a crossroad, a village square, and a "Main Street"

- Provide for safe and accessible drop-offs

- Provide for clarity of circulation

- Use simple loop configurations to minimize the "I'm lost" syndrome

MEMORABLE PLACES

- Create multiple scales and well-proportioned spaces, some comfortable for individuals, others for small groups

- Allow for linked activities and flexibility of use

- Design the entire facility in a comfortable way—one that promotes the formation of good, long-lasting memories

TECHNOLOGY AND INFRASTRUCTURE

- Provide adequate infrastructure for high-speed, broadband communications

- Anticipate the coming wireless revolution, providing convenient access unencumbered by plug-ins

- Incorporate federally mandated firewalling standards

- Consider high-resolution monitors for large-group Internet viewing

- Consider high-resolution readers for textbook download/display

- Consider acoustical aids for hearing-impaired students in electronic presentation spaces (computer labs, language labs)

- Incorporate space for portal management office

- Incorporate space for repair and disbursement of equipment and software downloads

SPECIAL EDUCATION (AND RELATED) NEEDS

- Take all relevant federal, state, and local laws and mandates into account

- Incorporate access aids for physically disabled students throughout

- Ensure that physical education and sports facilities allow for disabled access

- Incorporate "refuge" spaces (for wheelchair-bound students) in corridors

- Provide Braille signage for visually impaired users

- Incorporate space for electric wheelchair recharging stations

- Provide adequate planning and placement team meeting space

- Provide conference space for anger management and dispute mediation

HEALTH, SAFETY, AND SECURITY

- Ensure superior indoor air quality and climate control

- Provide for safe drop off, storage, and pick up of coats, musical instruments, other personal belongings (laptops, etc.)

- Provide appropriate, adequate lighting throughout

- Integrate ID card and smart/debit card systems

- Consider and select from range of electronic security technologies; anticipate possible use of facial recognition or other ID technology

The design process is an *educative* process for all the participants. At its best, it encourages *attention to detail* in the following areas:

- Understanding of building materials

- Appreciation for cost/value relationship

- Care about maintenance and operations

Fletcher Thompson's design approach is intentionally geared toward fostering this attention to detail. For example, architects and engineers typically evaluate both first-time cost and long-term performance when selecting and recommending building systems and products to the building committee and building users. We present only time-tested and thoroughly researched options to the decision-makers, and we frequently provide samples for more extensive testing to maintenance personnel prior to finalizing any decisions. This process affords building committees the opportunity to make informed decisions. Economy and design are not mutually exclusive; they are balanced through "value." Through the creative combination of commonly available, durable materials and carefully selected colors, an exciting design can be produced at minimal cost.

COLLABORATION

The beginning of a project provides the rare opportunity to make sure that the problems are correctly identified and that they will be creatively solved. The beginning of a project also provides an opportunity for soliciting input into the design and planning activities from the entire community of users. A new high school facility is certain to have quite a diverse set of *stakeholders*. Stakeholders are likely to include the following (and possibly others):

- Students

- Building committee members

- The board of education

- The superintendent and district administrators

- Municipal government agencies and officials

- The principal and school administrators

- Faculty and staff

- Parents

- Taxpayers

- Community groups

- Community leaders

Because of this diversity, we utilize an integrative process that includes workshops designed to promote the stakeholders' active participation. The goal of this collaborative process is to achieve "buy-in" on the part of all participants. Sharing the "authorship" of the project strengthens the sense of community and contributes to a successful building project.

Ensuring that the needs of the entire community of users are met requires the following:

- An interactive process involving all stakeholders

- An open exchange of ideas with workshops and focus groups

- An emphasis on *listening* to what is being said

- Establishing a common frame of reference

- Gaining consensus regarding the educational program

- Establishing a vocabulary of materials and furnishings

- Early identification of key milestones

- Previewing all information prior to design review and progress meetings so timely decisions can be made

- Ongoing dialogue about design alternatives

- Balancing design goals with budget criteria throughout project development

- Continuity of the core team to ensure successful implementation of ideas from design through construction

A series of study tools and deliverables, including the following, keeps decision-makers informed:

- Specific meeting agendas, meeting minutes, and monthly status reports

- 2-D diagrams and computer-generated 3-D images to document key programmatic relationships

- Simplistic models for critical design issues

- Bubble diagrams and conceptual drawings

- Image boards

- Site visits to comparable facilities

- Samples to discuss materials and aesthetic considerations (e.g., color consistency)

- System diagrams to ensure constructability, meet code requirements, and anticipate maintenance issues

- Design plans at all key milestones

- Presentation materials and renderings

PROJECT MANAGEMENT

Throughout the design and construction process, thousands of decisions are made that affect the quality, cost, and completion date of the final product. To successfully manage a project and communicate information to the members of the architectural team in a timely fashion, Fletcher Thompson utilizes customized project management tools, including a *Task Schedule* and a *Master Control Budget*. These tools help answer the important questions:

- What is to be done?

- Who will complete the task?

- When must it be done?

- How much will it cost?

- What happens if work isn't completed on time?

Task Schedule. The Task Schedule lists and schedules tasks to be accomplished throughout the project process. This allows team members to remain focused on the big picture while clarifying the steps necessary to get there.

Meeting the aggressive schedule imposed on a school construction project necessitates a clear and organized decision-making process. The Task Schedule shows when all the necessary decisions must be made in order to meet project goals.

One of the first tasks on the Schedule is the *Project Kick-Off Workshop*. In this meeting, the roles and responsibilities of all team members are established and the decision-making process is defined and agreed to. This consensus is critical to ensure the seamless flow of information and approvals necessary to move the project forward expeditiously.

The Schedule is a dynamic document that also tracks the tasks as work progresses, allowing for proactive management to keep the project on schedule to meet the project's goals.

The sample Task Schedule included on the following page shows the major milestones that would occur in virtually any school construction project. Of course, such schedules are tailored, expanded, and developed for specific projects and their integral components, incorporating the input of all the project team members.

Sample Detailed Task Schedule

PHASES & TASKS	MARCH, 2001				APRIL				MAY				JUNE			
	3/3	3/10	3/17	3/24	3/31	4/7	4/14	4/21	4/28	5/5	5/12	5/19	5/26	6/2	6/9	6/16	6/23

SUMMARY
PHASE 1 - Data Collection and Review
PHASE 2 - Program Review
PHASE 3 - Building Evaluations
PHASE 4 - Planning
PHASE 5 - Approvals

PHASE 1 - Data Collection and Review
Task 1.1   *Project Kick-Off - Workshop No. 1*
    Building Committee interview
    Outline goals
    Set meeting schedule
    Establish lines of communication
Task 1.2   *Existing Conditions Documentation*
    Assemble and review existing documentation
    Database existing documentation (Optional)
Task 1.3   *Existing Data Review*
    Review of existing facility reports
    Review of local code reports
    Review of P&Z and wetlands regulations
    Review demographic reports
    Review enrollment projections
    Review school capacity recommendations

PHASE 2 - Program Review
Task 2.1   *Programming Cycle No. 1*
    Review Educational Specifications
    Review preliminary program objectives
Task 2.2   *Workshop No. 2*
    Review with Building Committee

PHASE 3 - Building Evaluations
Task 3.1   *Site Analyses*
    Review facility site layouts
    Document site layouts
Task 3.2   *Building Inspections*
    Visit school facilities
    Document field visits
Task 3.3   *Building Evaluations*
    Evaluate expansion issues at each facility
Task 3.4   *Infrastructure Analyses*
    Review building infrastructure/MEP reports
    Summarize infrastructure/MEP capability
Task 3.5   *Technology Analyses*
    Summarize tech infrastructure capability
Task 3.6   *Code Analyses*
    Review life safety and accessibility reports
    Summarize life safety and accessibility issues
Task 3.7   *Workshop No. 3*
    Review findings with Building Committee

PHASE 4 - Planning
Task 4.1   *Planning Cycle No. 1*
    Develop concepts
Task 4.2   *Workshops No. 4 through 6*
    Review conceptual planning options
    Select preferred planning options

Master Control Budget. Fletcher Thompson maintains a high level of commitment to managing the cost of its projects throughout the design process. To ensure that the budget reflects the most up-to-date and accurate cost data available, we typically draw from the firm's historical construction cost database, reference published cost-estimating resources, and seek the help of regional estimating experts in both general construction and mechanical and electrical trades to adjust the unit costs used in our estimates. Doing so allows us to be sensitive and responsive to the cost control side of the design equation while still being able to develop highly creative and exciting solutions to a community's needs.

Success in cost control starts with the development and ongoing refinement of a realistic and comprehensive project budget. The Master Control Budget that we have developed not only lists a project's "Capital Construction Costs" but also includes "Other Capital Costs" (i.e., "soft" costs) and "Expenses." (Examples of these kinds of costs include architectural and engineering fees, testing, special inspectors' fees, moving and storage, bid printing and advertising, renderings, models, computer-generated "fly-throughs," and construction management.) Building committees find this to be a valuable tool for continually evaluating and managing the total cost of their projects.

Like the detailed Task Schedule, the Master Control Budget is a *dynamic* document that tracks costs as work progresses and is further defined. This framework facilitates timely, proactive adjustments to keep the project within its budget guidelines. The sample Master Control Budget included here would, of course, be customized for a specific project.

MASTER CONTROL BUDGET

	Quantity	Units	Cost/SF	Total	Eligible Cost	32.00%
I. CAPITAL CONSTRUCTION COSTS (HARD COSTS)						
1.1 Site Development		SF		$	$	
New Construction		SF		$	$	%
Field Repair				$	$	%
1.2 Off Site Improvements				$		%
1.3 Building Construction				$	$	
New Construction		SF		$	$	
Lower Level		SF		$		
Level Two		SF		$		
Level Three		SF		$		
Renovations		SF		$	$	
Lower Level				$		
Level Two				$		
Level Three				$	$	%
1.4 Change Order Allowance	%			$	$	%
1.5 Contingency	%			$	$	%
1.6 CM Fees/Reimbursables	%			$	$	%
SUBTOTAL CAPITAL CONSTRUCTION COSTS				$	$	%
II. OTHER CAPITAL COSTS						
2.1 Land Acquisition				$	$	%
2.2 Furniture and Furnishings		student		$	$	%
2.3 Computer Station Hardware		each		$	$	%
2.4 Front End Equipment, Servers				$	$	%
2.5 Telephone, Computer Wiring				$		%
2.6 TV Distribution Wiring				$	$	%
2.7 Security System Wiring				$	$	%
2.8 Miscellaneous Equipment				$	$	%
SUBTOTAL OTHER CAPITAL COSTS			$	$	$	%
III. EXPENSES (SOFT COSTS)						
3.1 Architectural and Engineering Fees				$	$	%
3.2 Specialty Consultants				$	$	%
3.3 Testing/Special Inspections				$	$	%
3.4 Surveys and Borings				$	$	%
3.5 Reimbursable Expenses				$	$	%
3.6 Full Time CA, Clerk of the Works				$	$	%
3.7 Moving and Storage				$	$	%
3.8 Bid Printing and Advertising				$	$	%
3.9 Rendering, Models				$	$	
SUBTOTAL OF EXPENSES			$	$	$	%
IV. BUDGET SUBTOTAL				$	$	
4.1 Legal, Admin, Bonding, Finance	%			$	$	%
V. PROJECT CONTINGENCY/ESCALATION	%			$	$	
VI. TOTAL PROJECT BUDGET				$	$	

Allowable Reimbursable Square Footage: sf
Adjustment for State "Allowable Square Footage Per Pupil" Calculation: %

To Be Paid By Town [   ]

Project Management: The Essential Components. Essential elements of Fletcher Thompson's project management process are summarized in the following lists:

TEAM ORGANIZATION

- Entire team committed to design excellence

- Key team members participate throughout the process

- One point of contact is designated

- Proper staff allocation and consultant participation are ensured

PROJECT MANAGEMENT

- Facilitate, record, and clarify team communications

- Define performance criteria and expectations

- Develop detailed Task Schedule with team

- Maintain all critical decision time frames

COST CONTROL

- Define scope of work commensurate with budget

- Maximize project value throughout the process

- Generate design and bid alternatives

- Develop and continually utilize Master Control Budget

QUALITY ASSURANCE

- Define excellence as a goal

- Make continuous product improvement efforts

- Use accurate and up-to-date data

- Provide bimonthly peer reviews

- Strong construction administration resources

- Specify mock-up evaluations and standards

As must be very clear by now, collaboration—in planning, design, and construction—is a very complicated process. To make sure that everything that needs to be covered actually gets covered, thorough checklists are essential tools. Multifaceted, problem-solving discussions too often focus on one problem (or a limited set of problems), to the detriment of other agenda items that also require close attention—and there's no way to keep on track without checklists, which can themselves be refined and added to as the process proceeds. The checklists we provide in this chapter aren't meant to be complete or exhaustive, but to show you the range of areas and specific action items that such checklists might very well include.

Chapter 6

A Case Study of Collaboration: East Lyme High School

East Lyme, Connecticut is located in the southeastern quadrant of the state, close to Long Island Sound, near New London and Salem. The East Lyme School district enrolled approximately 2,500 students and the Salem School district approximately 1,000 in the 1997–1998 school year. In 1997, a Vision Committee was formed to look at the possibility of renovating East Lyme High School and expanding its capacity from 1,000 to 1,500 students, enabling it to house the grades 9–12 population from both districts. The committee was made up of board of education representatives from each town, students from East Lyme High School, and a number of townspeople. The committee concluded that a high school consolidation/renovation/expansion project made sense: not only would it meet existing needs, but state reimbursements for such a project would rise from approximately 50 percent (if each town were to renovate its own existing high school) to 69 percent under the regionalized reimbursement formula.

Shortly after the Vision Committee reported its findings (see the Vision statement, below), a Development Committee was formed. (The East Lyme process was unusual in that each stage of the process was carefully named.) Though the Development Committee included many of the same people, the superintendent of schools and the East Lyme High School principal also became active members. Fletcher-Thompson, Inc., was hired to design the renovation/expansion of East Lyme High.

Working under the direction of the Development Committee—and working from the vision laid out by the Vision Committee—the architect was asked to develop an educational specification. Shortly after receiving that instruction, Fletcher Thompson began the process of databasing the school and meeting with staff to determine programming. A specification and then a conceptual design were developed, and the project was put to a referendum vote. In campaigning for the referendum, the district followed Fletcher Thompson's recommendations (summarized in Chapter 15 of the present book). The question regarding whether the renovated school should have a swimming pool (which would account for $2 million of the $16 million allocated for the project) appeared as a separate question on the referendum ballot.

Because the rationale for the project was so clear, voters approved both the renovation/expansion and the new swimming pool. In large measure, passage came as a result of the extensive work done by the Vision Committee, which had so carefully outlined the benefits of the project; by the Development Committee, which had reviewed and participated in the development of conceptual solutions; and by Fletcher Thompson, which had developed detailed educational specifications based on the staff interview process.

Immediately after passage of the referendum, a building committee was formed to put together the nuts and bolts of the actual project and see it through to completion. Interestingly, the three committees—known affectionately as the "dreamers" (the Vision Committee), the "schemers" (the

Development Committee), and the "doers" (the Building Committee)—never went away. Each group, in one form or another, tried to influence the other, and at times it was a little unclear which committee would make the required decisions.

Although some people complained that "too many cooks were spoiling the broth," what was in fact happening was that most decisions were getting an extremely thorough review. The taxpayers, as a result, got a feeling that the voters of Salem and of East Lyme were in control. Extensive collaboration was instilling confidence in the process.

Perhaps the best example of collaborative thinking and collaborative persuasion was exhibited by a fourth committee; the Pool Committee. Leaving no stone unturned, this committee presented usage and cost figures to any group that would listen, especially the Board of Education and the Building Committee. Arguing that the swimming pool should serve young and old alike, and projecting that its operational cost could be more than offset by fees charged for its use, the Pool Committee swayed sentiment in favor of the pool. By 1999, the completed pool was already fully scheduled and able to pay its own way operationally.

As a result of the renovation/expansion, East Lyme High School now offers an improved curricular program and flexibility in accommodating enrollment. Moreover, the high school enjoys the support of the entire community. The price of the impressive result was the time and energy allocated to collaboration. This case study illustrates that extensive, ongoing collaboration, supported by an architectural firm, can pay off.

The following document, prepared by the Vision Committee, was the touchstone of the entire process:

A VISION OF THE EAST LYME HIGH SCHOOL ADDITION SUBMITTED BY THE VISION COMMITTEE

East Lyme High School embodies the mission statement of the East Lyme Public Schools: "to enable each student to learn the information and skills necessary to be a productive member of our rapidly changing society." Our academic and extracurricular programs must enable all of our students to gain the academic, emotional, and social skills necessary to live purposeful and satisfying lives in an ever-changing world.

Future students will learn in a different manner from today's students. They will find, analyze, apply, and evaluate information with a teacher acting as a facilitator. Education for the new millennium will emphasize both process and product. Students must have an environment that allows them to succeed in these higher order tasks as well as an environment that allows for student

movement and teacher flexibility. The traditional classroom along with traditional teaching styles must change to enable students to demonstrate their new learning.

Space will need to be flexible to meet the needs of individuals, small groups, and full class presentations. In every space, access to information will be paramount. Each space must accommodate present as well as emerging technologies and be readily updated. Integrated or cross-discipline curriculum will be more and more common. Team teaching of courses and units will necessitate spaces that can accommodate varied uses. The ability to change the configuration of a facility as the needs of students change must be an integral part of the new construction.

For students to accomplish their learning objectives, they must physically be in many places for longer periods of time than traditional teaching methods demanded. The space must be aesthetically pleasing, adequately lit, and emotionally pleasing to maximize student learning.

Mathematics and science learning have a great potential for cross-disciplinary opportunities. These core curriculum areas and other related areas must be located in close proximity to one another to accelerate integration of instruction and enable teachers from different areas to communicate more easily with each other. Science classrooms must integrate data acquisition and analysis technology, instructional areas, and lab areas into one space. Science labs must be adaptable to change the arrangement and location of lab and technology sites as curriculum, methodology, and technology change.

The center of the curricular program is our library/media center. This area will continue to be the hub of the curricular wheel. The library must have adequate technology within the library/media center and be capable of being accessed from any place within the building or from the outside communities of Salem and East Lyme. Adequately wired data, satellite retrieval, mobile video conferencing units, and other information systems must be an integral part of the knowledge retrieval system of the library/media center and presented in a way they are readily accessible to the students. Our library must possess natural light and be well supported with windows, glass, and lighting. It should be in a central location and project dynamic architectural details that set it apart from every other area of the building. Technology should be liberally utilized throughout the library.

The school should also provide increasingly challenging learning opportunities in the arts. This area of human development demands adequate facilities that will provide our students with the most modern access and experiences in these areas. The building should provide facilities that enable students to perform and study without serious limitation of space, light, or acoustics. The performing areas should have an auditorium that possesses modern sound and lighting systems, as well as adequate dressing, storage, orchestra

pit, and seating facilities. The auditorium should be a first-class facility that can accommodate professional levels of performances. The music and art areas must be of adequate size and number to emphasize the importance of the arts to our students. Storage, performance, working, rehearsal, and dressing space must be of a size to accommodate the curricular and extracurricular programs.

In addition, the programs at East Lyme High School will continue to demand the rapid socialization and nurturing of students in their pre-college and pre-vocational years. New construction must provide the opportunities for students to interact with peers and adults in constructive manners. Common areas of the building must project an atmosphere of comfort, openness, and light. Students should feel that these areas are to be utilized for student events and socialization with peers as well as their standard functions.

Specifically, light and environmental effects must be a consideration in all areas of the building. There should be apparent natural and warm lighting throughout the building. Cost saving and functional energy efficiencies (HVAC) must be incorporated in the design. The school should have an open and welcoming atmosphere. The entryway should communicate a spirit of openness and responsibility. Students and teachers must feel that it is their home for learning and growing and be comfortable functioning in it.

Hallways should also project openness. Natural light should be a consideration in all hallways. Lockers should be one side of the hallway only. Student galleries, display areas, and study areas need to be integrated with the corridors of the building.

Administrative offices and support services offices should be spread throughout the building. The office of the principal and main reception area should reflect openness and light. The office of the principal should be adjacent to the high school entrance. Assistant principals will be housed in office areas with grade-level coordinators and secretaries. These offices will be in separate parts of the building.

The cafeteria should reflect a feeling of comfort and light. It should be designed as a student union center that encourages student gatherings. It should be able to accommodate food courts that can change over time. The cafeteria/union must be multipurpose and have a variety of seating types and designs. This area of the building should try to capture the spirit of student/teacher teams that continually work together.

In terms of technology there should be a seamless integration of the district and regional recommendations. On-line technology that enables all teachers and students to communicate with each other must be achieved as well as sufficient access to databases. Infrastructure wiring must be flexible, modular, accessible, and capable of supporting high bandwidths. All wiring must try to project the needs of the building at least ten years into the future

and be easily accessible for future upgrades. Classrooms should be flexible enough to handle multiple activities and group work. They should be large enough to accommodate student workstations, long tables, or desks as determined by teachers. Each classroom should have storage areas that are adequate for curriculum uses. Classrooms should be well lighted and windowed to enable students and teachers to create an environment of openness and light. Mini-theaters or large instructional spaces must be available for all departments. Two or three of these areas should be integrated throughout the building. Technology should be integrated in every classroom space with data drops for all students and teachers. Televisions and telephones are also a necessity in each classroom.

Teacher workspace should be adequate to provide each curriculum area with sufficient space that encourages innovative teacher instruction. Space must be able to be divided into large and small group areas to facilitate teacher/teacher and teacher/student interactions. Multiple publishing centers equipped with computers, scanners, copy machines, and state-of-the-art equipment should be available.

The design of the building should reflect present and future maintenance and custodial needs. Materials and architectural designs must enable the custodial staff to maintain the building in an economical and efficient manner. The high school appearance must reflect the positive work of teachers and students to the community throughout its building life. The improvements should extend to areas of the existing structure to ensure a pleasant and bright work area for all faculty and students. The cosmetic updates should also serve to provide a smooth transition to the addition producing a cohesive appearance of the old and new.

In addition to regular classrooms, some rooms must be capable of functioning as general computer and technology rooms. These rooms must be able to adapt to many future uses as needs and technology change.

The addition and renovations must also enhance the campus atmosphere of the facility. Exterior courtyards, patios, and walks should project an atmosphere of orderliness and cleanliness. The traffic flow and parking should be redesigned to provide an efficient use of parking facilities and entrance into the building. Plantings and shrubbery must be environmentally sound and provide ease of upkeep and appearance throughout the courtyards and walkways.

Part III: The High School of the Future

Chapter 7

The High School of the Future: General Principles

All discussion of educational specifications for the high school of the future must begin with an understanding of the general principles. All requests for space and all future program development should be built upon them.

At the heart of the general principles are three foundation blocks, which are at the base of all requests for space described in the educational specifications:

- Personalization

- Flexibility

- Technology

The general principles are as follows:

To Build a Learning Community

- *Personalization*

   The goal of the high school of the future should be to create an environment in which anonymity is banished. Every student will have an adult staff member with whom she/he can talk on a regular and timely basis. With respect to class size, attention needs to be paid to keeping student/teacher ratios low.

- *Spaces are needed where staff can converse with students, with each other, and with parents; where students can confer with other students; and where parents can meet and interact with other parents*

   Staff offices, student learning centers, shared departmental work rooms, the student assembly/parent community room, and the student commons are spaces where such communication can occur.

- *Centers for student learning throughout the school*

   No student should "fall through the cracks" and student learning centers are a major vehicle for achieving this goal. These areas, shared among departments, will provide space where teachers can give academic support to all students, individually and in small groups, as well as venues for close teacher/student interaction.

To Build a Dynamic Curriculum to Enhance Student Learning

• *Technology in every classroom*

• *Classrooms that support diverse instructional strategies*

Classrooms must be appropriately sized and shaped to enable teachers to work with an entire class of students, with groups of classes for special presentations, and with individual or small groups of students working together.

• *Space for teachers to collaborate with each other*

Shared departmental workrooms and shared student learning centers will help to encourage discussions and planning among departments, leading to greater collaboration. The regular opportunity to talk informally with members of other, related departments does not currently exist. Workrooms and learning centers should be shared by the English and social studies departments and by the math and science departments.

To Promote Excellence in Student Achievement

• *Quiet work areas for teachers and students*

• *Library/media center for large- and small-group instruction and individual study*

• *Technological resources for staff and students*

• *Flexible classrooms large enough to accommodate large-group instruction and student-directed learning in small groups*

Classrooms and hallways need to be flexibly designed so that students can work individually or in small groups, or so that two classes can be grouped together. Every room, common area, and office will be wired for technology. Students in the high school of the future will have all wireless laptop computers that they will use in classrooms and elsewhere, doing research via the Internet. All teachers will have websites, and teachers will communicate directly with students and parents at home through email.

To Serve the Needs of Diverse Learners

• *Learning areas that foster the use of a variety of instructional strategies that match the needs of individual learners.*

Students have unique strengths and weaknesses; they possess different and differing interests. The high school of the future must provide appropriate learning environments for all its students.

- *Space for instructional and noninstructional student support services*

  The student cafeteria/commons area should provide space for students to relax and talk to each other. The student assembly/ parent community room should provide an area for student government activities, as well as a place where parents can discuss school and community concerns among themselves or with members of the staff. The more parents are aware of and involved in the activities of the school, the more effective the school becomes.

To Ensure Flexibility

- *Classrooms and other learning areas must be able to be used in different ways to reflect changes in curriculum, technology, educational research and/or board of education policy*

  We know that a dynamic curriculum responds to developments in educational research, to the demands of the community, to changes in board of education policy, and to changes in technology. The educational specifications are designed such that the building will accommodate a changing curriculum, changes in program or daily schedule, or graduation requirement modifications.

To Promote a Comfortable and Healthy Environment

- *An HVAC system that provides adequate heat, ventilation, and air-conditioning*

- *Adequate storage space*

- *Effective communication systems*

- *Full compliance with the ADA, OSHA, and local fire department requirements*

  To be effective, a facility must provide for the safety, health, and comfort of all its occupants.

Chapter 8

The High School of the Future: Design Requirements for Specific Curricular Areas

The set of high school educational specifications that follows is generic and must be fine-tuned for a particular community and a particular number of enrolled students, but we believe it presents a good model on which to base design requirements for the high school of the future in communities around the country. (The specs given here are largely adapted from specs prepared for the renovation of the Staples High School, Westport, Connecticut; used by permission.)

In the high school of the future, it is vital that for every student there is at least one adult who knows that student well and with whom that student feels comfortable talking. One way to achieve this goal is to limit the number of students for whom each teacher is responsible during any one semester.

Among the staff, we need to balance the need for departmental and interdepartmental collaboration with the necessity for staff to have private, quiet, and secure places to confer with students and with parents, plan lessons, and do the necessary work required by the teaching profession. Shared student learning centers and departmental workrooms would give teachers within a department, and from different departments, the opportunity to talk about their work on a regular, informal basis, and this will provide a greater impetus for intra- and interdepartmental collaboration. At the same time, teachers need office space so that they can give their undivided attention, privately, to a student and/or parents as they discuss personal issues, review papers or other written work, or just to do the important job of getting to know students.

To optimize the learning-teaching environment, the high school of the future requires a state-of-the-art environmental and systems design that allows flexibility and promotes integration of technology throughout the educational program. All classrooms and offices should be wired for electronic data retrieval. There should be an ample number of outlets to support computers and technology. Classrooms and other workspaces should be wired for voice and video. Designated classrooms will have computer network "drops" to support a LAN of a minimum of 10 to 15 computers, distributed around a room and networked to an instructional server, the library media server, and the administration server, or comparable wireless networking capabilities. All classrooms also will be wired for a sound field amplification system.

All classrooms, conference rooms, department centers, the cafeteria, certain hallways, and the library/media center should have wall-mounted projection screens. Each classroom will have a wall-mounted television monitor and recording and playback capability. A telephone and speaker that provide public address capability, emergency outside-line access, and internal private communications must link each teaching space and workspace. There will be zoned heating and air conditioning throughout the school facility. All instructional spaces will include operable windows with screens and will have access to natural light and outside-air ventilation. In order to enhance the flexibility of room use, several rooms in each of the core academic areas should have flexible partitions or movable walls to enable teachers to work with larger numbers of students and to promote collaborative teaching.

Every consideration should be given to designing hallway and classroom space creatively to accommodate small-group work. Carpeted areas could be created in bay windows in classrooms to be used by breakout groups. Doors and walls leading to doors could be angled so that small benches would be available for small-group work.

Each classroom should have adequate, secure, lockable storage space for instructional materials, equipment, supplies, and student files. Departments will require sufficient bookrooms and storage space to house audiovisual and electronic media equipment. Department workrooms will be provided with a sink, cabinetry, and shelving. Sixteen-foot marker boards or blackboards should be installed in each teaching space. Shared department workrooms should be spacious enough to hold small group meetings.

Where possible, students should have access to the state internet backbone (known in Connecticut as State Internet II) to access virtual library resources and higher education distance learning opportunities.

Academics

Language Arts

1.   Program Objectives

Federal language arts standards mandate that students, by the end of 12th grade, should have developed proficiency, confidence, and fluency in reading, writing, listening, speaking and viewing to meet the literacy demands of the 21st century.

Specifically, students should be able to read and respond in personal, literal, critical, and evaluative ways to literary, informational, and persuasive texts. They should also produce written, oral, and visual texts to express, develop, and substantiate ideas and experiences. Students will use the language arts to explore and respond to classic and contemporary texts from many cultural and historical periods. They should also be able to recognize their own strengths and weaknesses in language arts.

2.   Activities

Activities to be housed include large- and small-group instruction and class work. Students will discuss, read, write, word process, present, dramatize, and conduct research, applying skills and content learned by utilizing material available in the classroom, as well as through the technological resources of voice, video, and print media.

Each classroom must be large enough to accommodate students working in small as well as large groups. Space must allow for teacher supervision of small groups, and acoustics must be appropriate to control the noise level. All students are also required to meet individually with teachers in conference. Therefore, a quiet space is necessary for each English teacher.

3.   Occupants

Persons to be housed include one English teacher and students. A special education teacher or paraprofessional or a reading or writing resource teacher may share instruction of small groups or individuals within the regular classroom.

Conferences with students represent a mandatory part of the instructional program. Each teacher needs a quiet space and a shared office to meet with students in conference, prepare lessons and assignments, evaluate papers and projects, conference with counselors and parents, and complete reports and grades. A student learning center is needed to provide additional time for one-on-one help for students who require more contact time with an English teacher.

4.   Furniture and Equipment

Furniture and equipment to be housed in each classroom include individual student worktables and chairs, a teacher worktable and chair, marker boards, a display board, open shelving, lockable cabinets with file drawers, and a lockable storage closet. In addition, each classroom contains a 30" wall-mounted "CTV" (computer-TV) monitor, which can display TV/video programming (DVD or VCR) or, when linked to the teacher's dockable laptop, website images and curriculum material for classroom instruction. Class rooms will be wired for high-speed, broadband Internet access (category 6+ or fiber) but also designed to accommodate wireless networking, ultimately permitting students to interact with images and information displayed on the CTV monitor from their own laptop computers.

Where possible, use of electronic textbooks and reference material should be anticipated, thereby reducing space needed for book storage.

Mathematics

1. Program Objectives

Students should become mathematical problem-solvers, learn to communiate and reason mathematically, learn to value mathematics, and develop confidence in their ability to do mathematics.

2. General Description

The high school mathematics program includes a range of offerings, including Applied Math (for students not quite ready for Algebra), Algebra, Geometry, Advanced Algebra, Pre-Calculus, Statistics (both regular and advanced placement), Calculus (both regular and advanced placement), and Multivariable Calculus for the most advanced math students. Although every mathematics course has a specific focus, in each course problems and explorations are introduced that cause students to revisit other strands of the mathematics curriculum, thereby highlighting the connections among different math topics and courses. Technology should be used extensively throughout the curriculum, enabling teachers to provide visual and physical components to illustrate abstract mathematical concepts, giving students opportunities to learn quickly and in depth. All courses should be applications-driven, meaning that mathematical skills and concepts are, to the greatest extent possible, taught in the context of real world situations. While it is still very important for students to be able to calculate and manipulate mathematical symbols, the focus is on the application of knowledge and skills.

3. Activities

Activities to be housed include large- and small-group instruction and class work. Students will discuss, read, write, compute, present, problem-solve, research, explore, and experiment. Students will regularly use technology, including advanced graphing calculators and computers. Teachers will provide computer access for their classes on a regular basis so that students can work with specialized mathematics software to carry out explorations and to do research on the Internet.

Each classroom must be large enough to accommodate students working in small as well as large groups. Space must allow for teacher supervision of small groups and acoustics must be appropriate to control the noise level.

4. Occupants

Persons to be housed include one mathematics teacher, students, and frequently a special education teacher or a reading or writing teacher. Shared office space is also required so that teachers have a place to work with students, conference with parents and special education resource teachers, and plan lessons. A student learning center is needed to provide additional time for one-on-one help for students who require more contact time with a math teacher.

5.   Furniture and Equipment

Furniture and equipment in each class should include student desks or worktables and chairs, teachers' desks and chairs, at least 50 feet of marker board per room, bulletin boards, two wall-mounted projection screens, open shelves, display space, and lockable storage closets. Laptop computers, advanced scientific calculators, laser disc players, video recorders, range finders, and a variety of manipulatives are just a few of the items our teachers use every day.

6.   Special Requirements

Because of the increasing dependence on computer technology, the mathematics curriculum requires access to computers for class-size sets of students to that they may work on a presentation or complete an exploration. All individual classrooms will be equipped with screens, and rooms will have access to natural light and ventilation.

Science

1. Program Objectives

The United States, through the National Science Education Standards, has set a national goal: the achievement of scientific literacy by all students. Scientific literacy allows students to participate effectively in the discussion of scientific issues that affect society and to strengthen skills that are important in everyday life (e.g., thinking critically, solving problems). Students must be expected to know and apply basic scientific knowledge in the life, physical, earth, and space sciences. Common themes of energy, matter, systems, change and continuity, and process and society run throughout this great diversity of subject matter.

Students should have many opportunities for inquiry and investigation: making observations, posing questions, using research, analyzing data, and proposing explanations. A critical combination of content and process is necessary to achieve these goals.

2. General Description

In general, ninth- and tenth-grade science classes can be offered in a computer lab setting, eliminating the need for expensive lab utilities and prep room facilities. Course for grades 11 and 12 will need the full "traditional" lab environment.

3. Activities

Activities to be housed include large- and small-group instruction, laboratory work (either virtual or hands-on), and class work. Students will discuss, read, write, compute, present, problem-solve, research, explore, and experiment.

4. Occupants

Persons to be housed include one science teacher, students, and frequently a special education teacher or a reading or writing teacher. Shared office space is also required so that teachers have a place to work with students, conference with parents and special education resource teachers, and plan lessons. A student learning center is needed to provide additional time for one-on-one help for students who require more contact time with a science teacher.

3.   Furniture and Equipment

Student lab work will be performed on an impermeable, chemical-resistant black epoxy resin top surface (or the equivalent) at standard height, allowing students to stand or sit on stools. For disabled students, each classroom must also be equipped with a portable lab station that is fully operational. At the 24 lab stations there should be a minimum of 24 gas jets, six deep sinks, 12 hot water and 12 cold water faucets, and 36 electrical outlets. Since each student may use up to 10 amps during some lab periods, three lab stations should be on 30-amp circuits. The sinks should have screened drains and a water trap that is chemical-resistant and easily cleaned.

Master gas and electrical shutoff should be provided in each room. Electrical outlets should have ground fault protection. Each room shall have a space for spill control materials and a chemical powder and eyewash that drains to an outlet. Each room should have the required safety equipment (eye-goggle sanitizing cabinet, fire extinguisher, fire blanket, and first aid kit).

All storage and closets will be lockable. Each room will have bulletin boards, wall space for charts, a wall- or ceiling-mounted projection screen, and a teacher demonstration area with some storage and access to all utilities—gas, electrical and water. There should be room for a standard two-student table beside each demonstration table. Each room needs space for two to six networked computers and printers with nearby terminal and electrical outlets. Each room needs two wall-mounted video monitors to allow all students to see at least one monitor clearly from his/her seat.

Each science room needs a minimum of three 4' x 8' high-quality whiteboards or marker boards, a bulletin board, a small blackboard on the wall near the classroom section of the room, a chemical fume hood, a full-size acid storage cabinet, and an upright or undercounter refrigerator. Rooms where advanced biology and chemistry classes are held require an explosion-proof refrigerator. The main work areas of both lab aides will have an explosion-proof refrigerator.

4.   Special Requirements

As science rooms are designed or renovated to meet the needs of the different science disciplines, each room will require individual design to allow for storage, counter space, and chart displays. Biology rooms need ample storage for microscopes, the variety of teaching supplies and chemicals, needed equipment, many models, goggles, and collections. Chemistry rooms need ample storage for student balances, the wide range of equipment and supplies used, models, and goggles. Earth science rooms need variable-size storage cabinets with adjustable shelving to house the wide range of equipment, supplies, goggles, and maps. Physics rooms need storage for the wide range of equipment and supplies used. Each lab station should have built-in student power supplies capable of delivering varying DC voltage to at least 25 volts and up to 10 amps, a 6-volt constant source, and an AC source that varies from 0 to 120 volts.

Science classes periodically need access to 24 computer stations, where students can individually use instructional software. Science classes will need to go to the library to use resources there. Physics and chemistry classrooms would profit by being located near math classrooms.

The greenhouse needs an independent heating system, a thermostat-controlled roof ventilation system, a thermostat-controlled heat/fan exhaust system placed at one end of the greenhouse, and the capacity for a controlled watering system. There will be a deep sink station along with another water source for hose hookups. The greenhouse will have adequate shelving for storage of supplies and workspace for planting.

Rooms need quiet ventilation appropriate for science rooms. Immediate fume removal should be available overhead in the lab areas. Some windows should open to the outside. These should be screened.

Each room or group of rooms requires separate prep and storage areas that support the science being taught close by. Each prep room has a combination of shelf, cabinet, and drawer storage. Each has at least one sink with access to gas, water, and electricity. Counter space must be adequate.

The prep areas used by the biology lab aide and chemistry lab aide need to be bigger to allow room for their office space and a fume hood. Each should contain a large sink with demineralizer, a dishwasher, and drying racks. Some counter space should have a 34-inch clearance to allow lab carts to slide underneath.

The biology prep area used by the biology lab aide needs space and lighting for plant growth and electrical outlets to run an aquarium. Adequate storage of preserved materials and commonly used biological supplies and equipment will be close by. This prep area should be on the same floor as the biology labs and close to them.

The chemistry prep area used by the chemistry lab aide needs adequate storage for commonly used supplies as well as ready access to storage facilities designed for acids, bases, and other chemicals used. This chemical storage area needs appropriate ventilation so that acid storage cabinets do not corrode. This prep area should be close to the chemistry classrooms and should be on the same floor. Science classroom/labs and prep areas should not be carpeted. They should be floored with non-skid vinyl tiles or a similar material.

Light controls should permit certain sections of the room to be lit while others remain dark. Shades or blinds should be durable and able to darken the entire room on any day, no matter how sunny.

Each room needs pegs or hooks for lab aprons near the student lab stations. If space is available, each room should contain an area of about 100 square feet to support student research projects.

Each new science room needs to be filled with supportive teaching materials, including microscopes, electronic balances, appropriate hardware, and glassware.

Social Studies

1. Program Objectives

The National Council for Social Studies has defined a vital social studies curriculum as one that, in the end, promotes civic competence, enabling young people to develop the ability to make informed and reasoned decisions as part of a culturally diverse and democratic society. For the high school for the future, we have used that definition and the ensuing standards to determine our objectives. Through an integrated study of the social sciences and humanities, students will achieve an understanding of the history of the Western world and the United States and that history's effects on their lives; an understanding of the histories and cultures of other regions of the world; an understanding of the operations of our representative government and their roles in it; and the ability to effectively communicate their ideas orally and in writing.

2. Activities

Activities to be housed include large- and small-group instruction and class work. Students will read, discuss, write, word process, present, dramatize, and conduct research, applying skills and content by utilizing materials available in the classroom as well as the technological resources of voice, video, and print media. The use of computers for Internet access and for writing and editing is extensive. Classrooms must provide access to computer use for all members of the class.

Each classroom must be large enough to accommodate students working in small as well as large groups. Since every course involves small-group work (approximately 50 percent of the class time), there must be enough space in each classroom for five to six groups of students to work effectively without interfering with each other. Classrooms must be flexible and dividable. Space, ventilation, and acoustics must be appropriate.

Since individual conferences with students are an integral part of the program, shared offices for teachers with a quiet space are an essential component of the department. Offices are also used to prepare lessons and assignments, evaluate papers and other student work, complete reports and grades, and do research.

There must be a workspace available for teachers; it should be wired for computers and other appropriate technology and outfitted with equipment necessary to prepare materials for lessons.

3. Occupants

Persons to be housed include one social studies teacher and, regularly, a special education teacher, writing and/or reading teacher, and students.

4. Furniture, Equipment

Furniture and equipment to be housed in each classroom include student worktables and chairs, a teacher worktable and chair, marker boards (24 feet), display boards, and recessed maps. There will be open shelving and lockable storage cabinets with file drawers.

Separate storage space for books and equipment is essential. Since each course uses a basic textbook and many courses use multiple sets of readings, the capacity of the book storage room must be 5,000 volumes.

5. Special Requirements

Two rooms should be available for presentations, lectures, or video presentations to multiple sections of the same course. These rooms should be dividable so they can also be used by single-section classes.

World Language

1. Program Objectives

According to the federal Standards for World Language Learning and the Classical Association of Connecticut, students' proficiency in a foreign language should result in a cluster of competencies. These include students' ability to communicate with people in other cultures while developing insight into their own language and culture. Students should also learn to act with greater awareness of themselves, of other cultures, and of their relationships to those cultures and to anticipate their participation in the global community and marketplace.

2. Activities

Activities to be housed include large- and small-group instruction and class work. All rooms should be located in the same area and have easy access to the world language labs, which are linked via network to a central, district-wide monitoring station providing instruction and supervision in multiple languages to students across the district. Rooms must have space for posting visual displays that reinforce the study of language and culture. Narrow display cases adjacent to language classrooms will display student work and artifacts from around the world.

A language learning center must be accessible to the students for small-group conversations, tutorial work, and enrichment activities, managed by teachers and advanced students of the language.

3. Occupants

Persons to be housed include one world language teacher and students, with regular access to a special education teacher. Each world language lab will have the capacity to house one class section with a maximum of 30 students, one teacher, and one aide at any given time.

4. Furniture and Equipment

Each classroom must have movable student furniture, a teacher worktable and chair, and whiteboards.

5.   Special Requirements

The world language lab, an all-inclusive multimedia learning center, requires 30 chairs and student carrels (each 36 inches wide) with sidewalls, equipped with computer interface, headphones, microphones, etc., and one master console/desk for each teacher. Two or three student carrels will be modified for use by disabled students.

Teachers will share office space but must have access to a small conference room. A storage room will house textbooks and workbooks (one of each for every student), video and audiotapes, DVDs, equipment, and supplies.

Fine and Performing Arts

Art

1. Program Objectives

The arts play a profound role in learning. Experiences in the arts are, in fact, basic to learning. The arts curriculum offers one way to formulate questions, construct knowledge, express meaning, and solve problems. The arts enhance language facility and the development of expressive skills. The arts inform and reform other areas of knowledge. Self-esteem, social awareness, critical thinking, sensitivity to others, sensitivity to one's environment, and problem-solving are all enhanced by an arts-infused approach to education.

2. Activities

Studios are needed to accommodate all art courses. Darkrooms are needed for black and white and color photography classes. A kiln room is needed for the ceramics component. A computer classroom is needed for computer graphics. A multipurpose classroom is needed for slide and video presentations and lectures, as well as for collaborative classes. Display cases for student work should be created throughout the school as well as an art exhibition space at the main entrance of the school and an additional art exhibition center in the art department.

3. Occupants

One art teacher is necessary for each 18-22 students per classroom.

4. Furniture and Equipment

Facilities needs and requirements for art classes are as varied as the individual course offerings. Rooms and equipment must be specialized to meet the needs of a diverse program. Because the program of study includes a broad diversity of art, media, and academic experiences, it is necessary that all the rooms have a studio-like atmosphere.

All art rooms, regardless of their assigned function, must have the following components: large spaces (The National Art Educators Association recommends a minimum of 55 square feet per student in all art classes, excluding storage and teacher's work space, and that it be flexible enough for individual or group activities); secured in-room storage; an adequate number (at least one per 10 students) of large sinks (at least 19" x 24" x 14") that are acid-resistant, equipped with heavy-duty drains with clay or plaster traps and hot and cold running water, fitted with mixing faucets, made of stainless steel or other materials that do not chip, crack, or break, and surrounded with waterproof work surfaces. In addition, general lighting should be planned so that shadows are reduced to a minimum in all parts of the room and that all students enjoy optimal visual conditions for doing their work.

Translucent skylights covering a minimum of 250 square feet are imperative. But there must also be a mechanism for controlling the light so that slides can be shown at any time, night or day. Acoustical treatments may be necessary to control sound levels when showing films. General and local ventilation systems are needed to remove fumes, odors, and dust and to make the air safe for students and teachers. At least one wall in every room should be covered with tackable material from floor to ceiling for displaying student work and visual aids. A large blackboard area is needed. Display areas such as shelves and cases should also be provided for three-dimensional work. These areas should be well lighted and equipped with multiple lighting plug-in tracks with movable spotlights. The rooms must be accessible to persons with physical disabilities. A resource library center (two 4' by 8' bookshelves) is needed in each room. Lockable storage facilities for materials must be adjacent to each art studio and must be large enough to store all the materials used in the activities of the studio (the NAEA recommends 400 square feet). Shelving in these storage areas should accommodate the diversity of art instructional materials.

Appropriate lockable and vented storage must be provided for flammable and combustible materials. Electrical outlets should be plentiful throughout the rooms to make the use of extension cords unnecessary. Appropriate storage cabinets, both horizontal and vertical, are needed for housing student work. Shared teachers' offices must also be adjacent to each art studio to allow for the supervision and safety of students as well as the security of materials.

The following requirements are related to specific courses offered:

Studio space for watercolor, oil, and acrylic painting and silkscreen printmaking should have 55 square feet per student in addition to storage for students' work in progress, portfolios, and materials. Facilities should accommodate equipment such as printing presses, drying racks, and easels. Care must be taken to provide adequate ventilation for the use of inks and solvents and for drying prints. Provisions must be made for the storage and disposal of hazardous materials.

Studio space for drawing should have 55 square feet per student in addition to storage for students' work in progress, portfolios, and materials.

Studio space for jewelry-making and other arts and crafts should have 55 square feet per student in addition to storage space for students' work. Metal casting stations and enamel and wax kilns are needed. Specific ventilation and an acid-resistant surface are needed for the jewelry bench.

Studio space for sculpture and ceramics should accommodate clay bins that are rustproof, leak-proof, airtight, and portable. Facilities should also accommodate special equipment such as potter's wheels and a damp box for storing work in progress. Appropriate ventilation must be provided for clay and glaze mixing.

There will be one darkroom for 25 students. It should have 25 workstations with enlargers, lenses and timers, and the electrical outlets to support them. Adequate counter spaces and sinks are needed. Darkrooms must meet stringent ventilation standards and other local safety standards such as eyewashes, etc. All drain piping in the darkroom must be acid-resistant.

The computer graphics room needs to be large enough to accommodate a computer workstation for each participant as well as printers, modems, laser disks, scanners, camcorders, a copying machine, and large layout tables. Computers, scanners, camcorders, and other high-tech video equipment are rapidly being adopted in art education. It is imperative that the computers be in a dust-free environment. This room will be shared with the music and theater departments.

The general purpose classroom, shared with the music and theater departments and accommodating 30 students, is needed for lectures, video presentations, and collaborative classes.

5. Special Requirements

There should be ample electrical outlets to support computers, technology, and dedicated art equipment in each room and a dedicated electrical system to accommodate kilns and other special equipment. Special ventilation and safety requirements must be accommodated in specific areas. Provisions for storage and removal of hazardous materials are necessary. Extremely high-quality lighting, both natural and artificial, is needed to accommodate the color/visual perception that is an essential component of art instruction. Sufficient space for lockable materials and student work storage is necessary. Ample student work display areas are needed in every room. Art exhibition centers shall be created at the main entrance of the school and in the art department.

Music

1. Program Objectives

Music education's mandate in contemporary American education, as stated by the Music Educator's National Conference, is to provide a varied, significant, and cumulative musical experience for every student. To accomplish this mandate, the high school of the future music experiences must be of a quality that enables students to establish working standards in their valuation of music, bring imaginative vision to all their experiences with music, attain the highest level of musical understanding of which they are capable, and gain significant proficiency in singing and playing an instrument to make it possible for them to be active participants in music throughout their lives.

2.   General Description

Students in grades 9 through 12 may elect a variety of classes in music. Vocal classes include Freshman Chorus, Chorale, A Cappella Choir, and independent voice classes. Band classes available are Freshman Band, Symphonic Band, and Jazz Ensemble. Orchestra classes should be available including Freshman String and Full Orchestra, Symphonic Orchestra, and Chamber Orchestra.

3.   Activities

The uniqueness of each of the large performing ensembles, as well as of the other, nonperformance classes, dictates a unique utilization of each proposed space. However, each of the rehearsal and classroom facilities should have 15 feet of blackboard space with music staff lines on the center third of the board and flag holders and tackboard above and 12 linear feet of tackable wall panels, each 8 feet high.

The vocal room will house the various vocal ensembles and voice classes. A large, acoustically appropriate space—one large enough to accommodate 120 students and chairs—is needed. The space should have a high ceiling and built-in risers. A grand piano, conductor's chair and podium, folio cabinets to hold music folders for every ensemble, and built-in, lockable stereo equipment are also needed. A secure storage facility, located adjacent to the vocal room, will house 120 choir robes, scenery and props, nine choral risers and back railings, and storage cabinets to accommodate 1,500 titles of choral music.

The band room, which will house the various levels of band and jazz band, should be an acoustically appropriate, high-ceilinged space large enough to accommodate 100 students. A lockable cabinet or closet to house current percussion equipment, folio cabinets to hold folders for all ensembles, conductor's chair and podium, and built-in and lockable stereo equipment and tuner are needed. In addition, lockable storage units to house student-owned instruments (ranging in size from flutes to tubas) are needed. A secure band storage facility adjacent to the band room will house all marching-band percussion instruments, electronic equipment for jazz, and storage cabinets to accommodate band music titles.

The orchestra room which will house the various levels of orchestra, should be an acoustically appropriate, high-ceilinged space large enough to accommodate 100 students. A lockable cabinet or closet to house current percussion equipment, a separate storage cabinet for string basses, folio cabinets to hold folders for all ensembles, a conductor's chair and podium, and built-in and lockable stereo equipment and tuner are needed. In addition, lockable storage units to house student-owned instruments (ranging in size from violins to string basses) are needed. A secure orchestra storage facility adjacent to the orchestra room will house nine acoustical shells and storage cabinets to accommodate titles of orchestra music.

Practice rooms of varying sizes (able to accommodate from four to ten students) will be used for small ensembles and sectionals. Each room should be equipped with a digital piano and computer.

The music/art/theatre computer lab/classroom will be a multidisciplinary, multipurpose room able to accommodate 30 students as well as accompanying computers and equipment for use in computer graphics, music theory, and light, sound, and recording engineering. It should be totally soundproof and be equipped with an intercom system feeding into the adjacent large ensemble room to facilitate the recording of musical groups.

All music teachers must have shared office space adjacent to their rehearsal rooms in order to supervise students and safeguard instruments. Office space should be roomy enough to accommodate conferences with parents and/or students and to enable teachers to prepare lessons and assignments, evaluate student work, and complete reports and grades and should provide space for research and for teachers' computers.

An office is needed for the district's music supervisor. The office must be large enough to accommodate conferences with students, parents, and/or teachers as well as to house research materials and personnel files. An additional office is needed for the district's music and fine arts secretary. It must be large enough to accommodate district files, fax machine, computer, and worktable. Storage must be made available for the district's instruments, ranging in size from flutes to string basses and tubas. The district's music library must also be stored in an area accessible to all music teachers. These areas must be in close proximity to each other and the music department since the secretary and supervisor are responsible for the security of the inventory.

The black box theater, a mid-size capacity theater, will be used for recitals, instrumental and vocal chamber concerts, and jazz concerts.

4. Occupants

Each of the rehearsal rooms will accommodate from 100 to 120 students and one teacher for the large ensembles. Approximately four instrumental teachers will direct the bands and orchestras and must have an equal number of teaching stations in which to deliver the small-group lesson programs. Office space must also be provided for them adjacent to their rehearsal facility. Approximately two vocal teachers will direct the vocal ensembles and must have an equal number of teaching stations in which to teach voice classes, theory, guitar, piano, and the collaborative classes planned. Shared office space must also be provided adjacent to their rehearsal facility.

5. Furniture and Equipment

Music is a specialized discipline and requires unique equipment. Instrumentalists require a special chair, e.g. the Wenger "musician," to facilitate good posture. Good quality, professional, black music stands are also necessary, as are conductors' chairs, podiums, stereo equipment, and pianos in all the rehearsal rooms. Electronic pianos are needed in all practice rooms. Wenger music filing cabinets (similar to the ones seen in doctor's offices) will enable teachers to store all their music in a relatively compact space. Individual lockers are needed in each of the instrumental rehearsal facilities to secure student instrument storage. Teachers' offices should have desks, computers, filing cabinets, bookcases, and a storage closet.

6. Special Requirements

The multipurpose classroom/computer room/recording room must be adjacent to one of the large rehearsal facilities and must be completely soundproof. Proximity to the auditorium is necessary, with access to both stage right and left. Interior accessibility to the lobby of the auditorium is also necessary. Proximity to exterior doors is needed for easy transportation of instruments and equipment.

Theater

1. Program Objective

The theater curriculum is built around the capabilities and character of older teenagers, who are generally able to understand relationships between people and groups of people, who are willing to learn about their own feelings regarding social mores, who are aware of society's impact on them, who are preparing to make life decisions, and who are developing the ability to project future social trends and to see the impact that an individual can have on society.

Thus, all students can learn from improvisational work, literary analysis of all types of dramatic literature, scene study aimed at production, formal full-length productions, workshops, and performances. Improvisational work should be the foundation for all types of learning about drama and theater. All other skills of self-expression and performance logically flow from the genuine responses elicited through improvisation.

While improvisation is fundamental, there are other skills that should be explicitly cultivated and improved: sensory and emotional awareness; recall and performance; use of rhythm and movement to express complex characterization, abstract qualities and the unity of ensemble playing; and use of oral communication skills such as articulation, variety, and timing. Competencies need to be developed in acting, directing, and all areas of stagecraft and management.

2. General Description

Currently, courses include Introduction to Theater, Advanced Theater, and Stagecraft.

3. Activities

All acting, directing, children's theater, and theater voice classes will take place in the black box theater. Theater Management and Playwriting will take place in the fine arts building multipurpose classroom. Theater makeup class will take place in the makeup room. Stagecraft will be housed in a separate technical theater space that will meet OSHA specifications for safety and ventilation. Sound, lighting, and video design and engineering will take place in the fine arts building computer classroom and auditorium. Costume design and fabrication will take place in the costume/sewing room. In addition to the sequence of elective classes described, there are main stage productions, which take place in the main auditorium. With the use of the black box theater and the increase in personnel, the number of studio productions can expand dramatically.

The drama and technical teachers must have office space in which to meet with students and/or parents in conference, prepare lessons and assignments, evaluate papers and other student work, and complete reports and grades.

4.   Occupants

One teacher and approximately 25 students will attend theater classes in the black box theater, fine arts multipurpose classroom, makeup room, and costume room. Main stage and black box theater productions may have as few as five or as many as 100 students participating, depending on the format chosen. These spaces will also house one to two acting teachers and one to two technical teachers as well as technical support personnel for costumes, scenery, art and graphics, publicity, communication, makeup, and other specialty areas.

5.   Furniture and Equipment

Theater is a specialized discipline. Therefore, each room is unique in its purpose and the equipment needed. A separate lighting grid and booth should be added to the black box theater. The black box theater should be a mid-size facility with a seating capacity of 200 to 225, movable stage and seating capabilities, and ample wing and fly space. Standard theater lighting and sound capabilities are necessary.

The costume room needs to have increased storage capacity as well as a sink, washer, dryer, and the electrical capacity to run all the equipment. The makeup room needs excellent theater lighting, large mirrors, cabinets to store cosmetics, and sinks. The stagecraft workroom must meet OSHA requirements, and its power equipment, electrical capacity, and ventilation system must meet local codes. Dedicated computers are needed for business and finance, lighting, and sound. Faculty offices must have desks, filing cabinets, bookshelves, storage closets, and computers.

6.   Special Requirements

All theater areas need to be located near the auditorium. Shower and bathroom facilities need to be located near the theater area. Separate electrical power and circuit breakers are needed for the stagecraft workshop and costume room.

Black Box Theater/Large Group Instruction-Lecture Room

1. Program Objective

The black box theater laboratory provides a small theater and music performance laboratory, capable of seating from 200 to 225 audience members. The facility would support both school and community events and activities.

The purpose of the large group instruction/lecture room is to provide space for student exhibitions and projects, including optional theatrical courses, for language arts activities and public speaking instruction, for specialized testing such as Advanced Placement tests, and for panel presentations for audiences larger than one class.

2. General Description

The program for the high school requires a rehearsal space for theater classes with a flexible stage and seating arrangements. The space will also serve as the studio production classroom. The studio will accommodate from 200 to 225 students, staff members, parents and/or visitors. Such space will serve the community for small group music and theater performances and other public gatherings.

Although most high school learning activities will continue to occur in regular classrooms, the high school program requires a large group instruction area, with tiered seating, for up to 150 students or adults. Departments will use this large group instruction area for presentations and other activities. Since this area will support two different functions (theater and large group instruction), flexibility is critical. Adolescents need a setting in which to develop and practice performance skills that is more intimate and less intimidating than the large auditorium. Numerous small groups developing their skills in the performing arts—such as chamber ensembles, jazz groups, vocal soloists and groups, and a variety of drama groups—will use this space.

This large group instruction room will also be used by the school district and the community for purposes like those just noted. It will also support staff development for the high school and subgroups of the high school's staff throughout the year.

3. Activities

Activities to be housed include student-run dramatic productions, play rehearsals, theater classes, and other traditional school meeting-place functions. The continuing education program will use this space on a regular and ongoing basis. Students will view, read, listen, present, dramatize, and perform, applying skills and content learned in the classroom.

4. Occupants

Persons to be housed include from 200 to 225 students, staff, and community members. The black box theater will be used for both school- and community-sponsored activities and events.

5. Furniture and Equipment

The black box theater should include a presentation area, which will accommodate both small- and intermediate-scale performances, sloped seating, a display screen, a television monitor, a public address system, lighting, and sound to support small concert and theater productions. The HVAC system will run efficiently and quietly.

Furniture and equipment to be housed include student chairs, tables, portable markerboards, display boards, a recessed projection screen, a wall-mounted TV monitor, and a lockable storage closet.

6. Special Requirements

The black box theater should be easily accessible by community members as well as by the school population. Disabled access is required. It must include adequate storage and preparation areas for sets and materials used in theater performances. Entrances and exits shall provide for the comfortable and safe coming and going of audiences and performers. The stage floor must be appropriate for dance movement and floor exercises.

Lighting and sound systems should be installed to support special presentations and performances. There should be easy access for outside community use after normal school hours.

Stagecraft

1. Program Objectives

The students should be able to demonstrate the application of the elements and principles of visual design to the specific problems encountered in stage design. Technical knowledge will be realized through workshop experiences, which combine theory and hands-on practice. Various scenic styles—realism, naturalism, minimalist/skeletal, etc.—will be studied as they apply to the production of a play and the director's concept.

2.   General Description

This course is designed to develop the knowledge and understanding of the aesthetic principles and skills essential to stage design. The course illustrates the complex interrelationships inherent in successful stage design.

Stage design embraces the total concept of the stage. It includes effects produced by the setting, stage properties, lighting, costumes, actors' makeup, and the positions and movement of the actors in time and space.

The major focus of this course is the role of the artist as a designer of the setting, costumes, makeup, and lighting. Since the purpose of these efforts is to enhance the effects of the play for the audience, the designer must know the production's intent and how the director and the actors will interpret it.

Through the visual aspects of the production, the designer's aim is to provide a specific mood or atmosphere and an illusion of the time and place of the action to enhance the objectives of the playwright and director.

Therefore, the study of stage sets includes both design and technical aspects. In addition to viewing slides and models, students participate in the construction of scenery for school plays and have the opportunity to work on lighting, sound, costume, and makeup.

3.   Activities

Activities include the study of historical set designs, the construction of theater sets, costume design, makeup design and application, and the design and execution of lighting and sound plots.

4.   Occupants

Persons to be housed include the technical drama teacher and support personnel, including lighting, sound, costume, and makeup designers. One teacher will be required for each 18 to 22 students.

5.   Furniture and Equipment

The theater workshop is a highly specialized facility. It combines a craftsman's workroom with a classroom facility. The main facility should be approximately 60' x 35' to accommodate 18 to 22 students and a teacher. Additional storage space is needed to secure sets, wood, paints, etc., away from this classroom. Large stationary woodworking equipment such as a table saw, band saw, and drill press is needed, as is portable equipment such as sanders, drills, and spray-painting equipment. Manual tools such as hammers, screw drivers, etc., are also needed. Several large sinks (at least 19" x 24" x 14") that are acid-resistant and equipped with heavy-duty drains and hot and cold running water and fitted with mixing faucets made of stainless steel are needed for cleanup. General and local ventilation systems to make the air safe for students and teachers are needed to remove fumes, odors, and airborne particles. Lockable storage facilities for portable power equipment and fire-rated cabinets for paint and other flammable materials are needed. Electrical outlets should be plentiful and located all around the room to make the use of extension cords unnecessary. A shared teachers' office should be located adjacent to this facility to allow for supervision and safety of students as well as the security of materials.

6.   Special Requirements

Large overhead doors are needed with access to the outside to allow for the delivery of lumber and other large supplies for set building. Provisions for storage and removal of hazardous materials are needed. A dedicated electrical system is required to accommodate stationary and portable power tools and other special equipment. Special ventilation and safety requirements must be adhered to. Lockable storage cabinets are needed for portable power and manual tools. A separate storage facility, large enough to accommodate sets, flats, wood, paints, and other materials, is also needed.

Physical Education/Athletics

1.   Program Objectives

The physical education program should allow all students to develop their physical capacities and capabilities in order to help them understand their strengths and weaknesses. The program must give them some experience with physical education modes such as dancing, volleyball, archery, and other activities. The athletics program is designed to give students an opportunity to develop and demonstrate strengths in locally recognized activities such as football, swimming, and so on.

2.   General Description/Activities

The facilities will accommodate physical education and athletic activities serving a total student population of 2,000. Below, facilities needs are broken down into those for physical education and those for athletics, though there is obviously overlap between the two.

Physical Education

- Three gymnasiums (6 full teaching areas) and/or fieldhouse

- Fitness center/weight training room

- Storage for all equipment (from balls to gymnastics equipment)

- Separate boys' and girls' locker rooms with toilet and shower facilities

- Bleachers sufficient to seat 1,500 students, faculty, and visitors

- Sound system

- Scoreboard with auto-timer

- Fields for outdoor sports (including archery, golf, baseball, softball, soccer, field hockey, lacrosse)

- Lighted football field, with bleachers and press box

- Tennis courts

- Swimming pool

Athletics

Provisions should be made for adequate indoor and outdoor space for the following sports. This space includes office/conferencing space for coaches and trainers, equipment storage, and space for practice sessions and competitions. The high school of the future also has a sports medicine/first aid suite.

•	Baseball	Boys'
•	Basketball	Boys' and Girls'
•	Cheerleading	Girls'
•	Cross Country	Boys' and Girls'
•	Fencing	Boys' and Girls'
•	Field Hockey	Girls'
•	Football	Boys'
•	Golf	Boys' and Girls'
•	Gymnastics	Girls'
•	Lacrosse	Boys'
•	Soccer	Boys' and Girls'
•	Softball	Girls'
•	Swimming	Boys' and Girls'
•	Tennis	Boys' and Girls'
•	Track and Field (indoor/outdoor)	Boys' and Girls'
•	Volleyball	Boys' and Girls'
•	Wrestling	Boys'

Chapter 9

The High School of the Future:
Conceptual Drawings

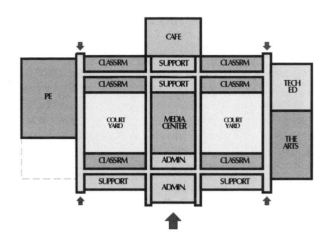

DIAGRAM STUDY A

- Department or fully integrated plan.
- Good distribution of students with ample circulation.
- Three distinct public entries and lobbies.
- Courtyards.
- Large visual mass.
- Poor future expansion capabilities.

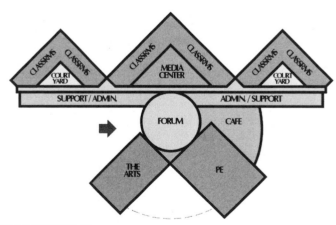

DIAGRAM STUDY B

- Department of fully integrated plan.
- Large centralized forum (public lobby).
- Good separation of public and private.
- Main Street organization plan.
- Good flexibility and expansion capabilities.

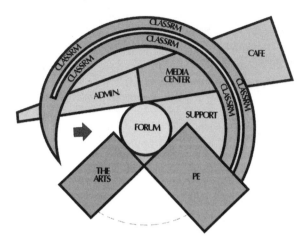

DIAGRAM STUDY C

- Department or fully integrated plan.
- Large centralized forum (public lobby).
- Small visual mass.
- Good flexibility.
- Poor future expansion capabilities.
- Good adjacencies and circulation.

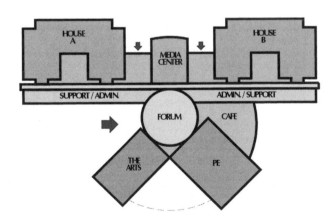

DIAGRAM STUDY D

- House plan.
- Large centralized forum (public lobby).
- Good separation of public and private.
- Main Street organization plan.
- Poor flexibility and future expansion capabilities.
- Smaller school within a school feeling.

Chapter 10

The High School of the Future: Achieving Balance in Design

As "finished" as they seem, the design requirements for specific curricular areas presented in Chapter 8 still represent a kind of "wish list" that may have to be pared to match budgetary realties—to be brought into line with what's actually affordable, given state reimbursement formulas and the community's own resources.

The actual design of the high school of the future involves achieving a balance between the square footages required to implement the program (as laid out in the specs) in each curricular area and the overall square footage per student, based on enrollment projections. Achieving that balance is equivalent to the process an arranger or conductor goes through when attempting to produce the right mix of instruments and instrumental sections in an orchestra—in other words, it's a delicate job, and getting the right mix may require a series of incremental adjustments.

Fletcher-Thompson, Inc., has developed a set of visual tools to make this process more comprehensible and easier to perform—for bringing the requirements outlined verbally in the specifications under a visual micro-scope. Before going on to the last part of this book—in which we turn our attention to some of the thornier issues influencing high school planning, design, and construction—let's look at two of these tools and examine their value.

SQUARE FOOTAGE PER STUDENT/BY PROGRAM AREA

For districts in states where reimbursements are based on square footage per student, it's important to gain some idea of net square footage first, and then to see how that square footage breaks down per student by program area. This is crucial to determining how much of each program area, as defined by the educational specification and the ballpark square footage figures calculated by the architect will be eligible for reimbursement. Figure 10.1 shows ranges of square footage per student by program area for a number of Fletcher Thompson–designed high schools in Connecticut, as well as for the high school of the future outlined in the sample specs in Chapter 8.

A visual tool like this—or one like Figure 10.2, which shows square footage per student for a hypothetical small high school—can be very useful as the building committee sets to the task of balancing programmatic needs with budgetary realities. Such diagrams make the relations among the various program areas (in terms of square feet, that is) immediately clear and make it easier to adjust square footages to achieve the right balance—one that meets programmatic needs while matching, as closely as possible, state reimbursement formulas.

Of course, such diagrams cannot by themselves tell you how much of a given space is likely to be reimbursed. For that, you'll have to use other sources of information and make judgments about how much can or cannot be sacrificed accordingly. For example, some states will allow full reimbursement for auditoriums that are sometimes used for democratic student assemblies (e.g., those that teach so-called higher-order thinking—"HOT"—skills); others cap reimbursements for auditorium space at 50 percent.

If you study Figure 10.1, on the following page, you'll notice that these Connecticut high schools vary pretty widely, especially in terms of the square footages per student in the areas of science, auditorium/assembly, and physical education. This, of course, raises another issue—that is, how far beyond state reimbursements a community is willing to go in providing the best possible educational facilities for its children. Obviously, these Connecticut schools, for whatever set of compelling reasons, made very different decisions on this score.

Figure 10.1 Average SF/Student by School

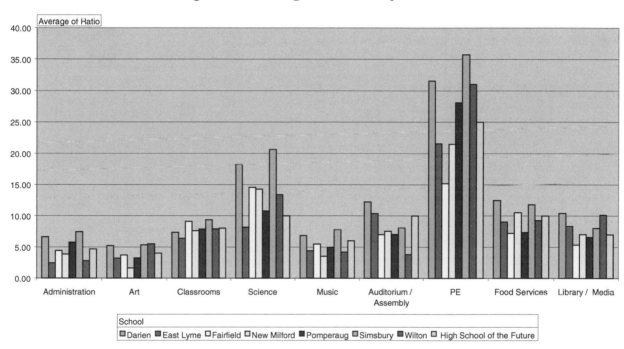

Figure 10.2 Square Footage per Student

Distribution for 95,558 Gross SF. / 600 Students

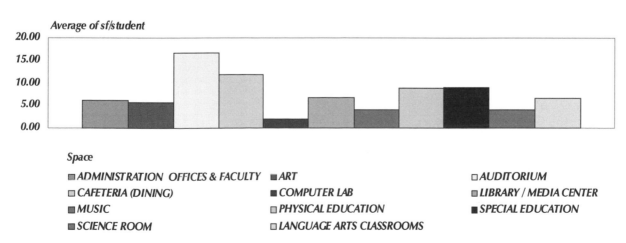

Part IV: Issues in High School Planning, Design, and Construction

Chapter 11

Ensuring Health and Comfort in the Indoor Environment

by Richard S. Oja, AIA

Among the most important considerations in new high school design and construction is ensuring a healthy, comfortable environment for all occupants—students, faculty, staff and administration, and visitors. Although this chapter speaks mainly of the indoor environment, it is important to remember that the "environment" is both the interior space defined by the building's physical structure and the surrounding outdoor environment, which can have a profound impact on what happens indoors.

The character of each of the elements of the indoor environment—the air, the lighting, the acoustics—affects our perception of the space as either safe and comfortable or unhealthy and unpleasant. Lighting levels, for example, must be appropriate to the task or activity. If the space is too bright, the glare may hamper our ability to read printed documents, computer screens, or video monitors. A space that is too dark may cause eyestrain; a dimly lit corridor may produce a feeling of being unsafe.

Acoustical properties, too, must be appropriate to the space and the activities that take place there. In certain spaces (for example, a performance space) a certain amount of reverberation, or "liveliness," may be desirable. In other spaces—a fully occupied cafeteria, say, where 400 students are having lunch—acoustical liveliness is undesirable, since the sounds, as they bounce around, mix and become a din. Conversely, if the all the surfaces are soft and porous, a room will seem hushed or dead. That might be appropriate in a library or media center but inappropriate in a music room or an auditorium.

The most important environment factor, however is the quality of the air we breathe. If, in a fully occupied room, the ventilation is inadequate and carbon dioxide (CO_2) levels rise above a certain point, the room feels stuffy, stale, and confining. We may feel drowsy or fatigued, and if the same room lacks windows or other visual access to daylight, the confining effect is even more severe. If the air is contaminated with pollutants such as volatile organic compounds (VOCs), which are frequently found in science labs, the odors can range from unpleasant to noxious and the effects can be toxic. If the temperature controls are entirely centralized, people will complain of being too hot or too cold even though sensors may indicate appropriate conditions.

Suffice it to say there are many factors that affect the indoor environment. In designing an ideal high school of the future we must be mindful of all of them.

GAS AND PARTICULATE POLLUTANTS

In general, poor IAQ—and the health-related problems it causes—can be traced to two sources:

- The pollutants themselves

- Transport mechanisms, or the manner by which pollutants move from the source to the occupant

It is important to remember that sensitivity to pollutants can vary greatly from individual to individual: what one person perceives as merely an unpleasant odor may very well induce an asthma attack or other debilitating reaction in another person.

Indoor air pollutants appear in two forms—gases and particles. Gases that are commonly implicated in IAQ problems include the following:

- CO_2, chiefly as a respiratory byproduct

- Combustion byproducts such as CO, nitrogen dioxide (NO_2), and PAH (polyaromatic hydrocarbon)

- Radon

- Volatile organic compounds (VOCs), chemical compounds that evaporate from a solid or liquid to a gas state at normal ambient conditions and that can be expelled from building materials (sometimes referred to as "off-gassing")

Particulate pollutants also belong to a number of different categories:

- Dust

- Bioaerosols, such as molds, mildew, fungus, bacteria, skin flakes and animal dander, and dust mites and their remains

- Microscopic fibers, such as asbestos or fiberglass fibers

The list of potential pollutants, which are often related to specific functions within the building, is a very long one. The preventive solutions list, on the other hand, is brief. Good design, appropriate budget to support the design, careful selection of materials, quality construction, and a sound maintenance program should yield a healthy, safe, and long-lasting building.

A LITTLE PROBLEM GROWS, AND GROWS, AND . . .

Each of a building's parts—its floor, its roof, its walls—is actually a *system* of components. This is important to understand because each of these systems is made up of various materials that can influence the indoor environment. It is also important to understand that, although we often think of buildings as static, they are in fact dynamic structures, subject to the effects of temperature changes, of wind and weather, and of ground settlement. Building materials expand and contract with heat and cold; they bear the force of wind, rain, and snow loading; and they sink or rise as the ground beneath the building shifts. This means a building is constantly moving—usually imperceptibly, but moving nonetheless. If allowances, such as control joints and expansion joints, are not made for these dynamic forces, the building will slowly self-destruct.

A wall system, for example, is made up several different materials. On the exterior face, a layer of brick veneer protects the underlying structure from the elements. Sandwiched between the interior surface and outer layers are insulation, studs, steel structure, sheathing, vapor retarders, and air barriers, depending on the design of the particular system. On the interior side there may be gypsum wallboard, plaster, tile, masonry, or a combination of these, as well as layers of paint or other, so-called high performance coatings.

Each of these materials and the way in which it is installed can influence the quality of the environment that it helps define. When properly selected and constructed, these systems become "transparent"—they are simply the walls, floors, and ceilings. However, if one or more of the components is incorrectly specified or haphazardly installed, the effect on the indoor environment can be devastating. An improperly located expansion or control joint may result in the cracking of the mortar joints in the brickwork, which can allow excessive amounts of water to infiltrate the wall, leading to the corrosion of structural components. This could lead to the breakdown of the sheathing materials, or the insulation layer could become saturated with moisture, canceling its insulating properties. And this, in turn, could allow cold exterior air to infiltrate the building, leading to condensation on the hidden surfaces of the interior finishes when the cold outside air meets the warm, moisture-laden indoor air. Before long, mold and mildew will grow on those moist surfaces and, if unchecked, will continue to spread along various pathways. Molds release spores into the breathing zone, and these are spread to other areas of the building by the HVAC system.

Let's continue to extrapolate this example: As the spores spread, students feel fatigued and experience headaches or eye irritation. They tell their parents about feeling sick in school, and faculty absences due to sickness increase. The school nurse reports a higher number of asthma-like episodes, and the administration is beset with complaints about air quality problems in the building. Students' ability to perform well declines, and the educational process is now compromised.

The building, designed to facilitate learning, has become its inhibitor. The school administration finds itself on the defensive as the teachers' association presents documentation of health problems and demands solutions for its members and as the town's taxpayers—who voted to fund the new school building—grow furious as they become aware of its significant indoor air quality problems. The anger is stoked by unsympathetic local television coverage and by newspaper reports and editorials, and parents organize and begin to refuse to send their children into the unhealthy building.

Several parents call the local health official, who is legally required to act on the problem. He contacts the superintendent of schools and demands more information. The administration calls in an IAQ expert to evaluate the situation—and quickly learns of the high cost of extensive testing. So the consultant is hired for a truncated study, conducts some limited air testing in a few of the rooms, and confirms that pollutants are present in levels higher than the department of health's recommended action levels. The superintendent turns to the architect for answers; the architect calls the engineer who designed the HVAC systems; the engineer calls the HVAC contractor who installed the systems, who in turn calls the general contractor. The GC, with nowhere left to turn, calls his insurance company and legal counsel. What has been a rapidly accelerating problem is about to get bogged down!

Of course, this is only an imaginary scenario—though an entirely possible one—but it demonstrates how a small problem, as minor as an improperly located control joint, can escalate into a town-wide controversy. Solutions to problems like this are frequently complex and expensive, involving the reconstruction of parts of a building and its systems.

THE SOLUTION IS PREVENTION

In designing and building a new high school, care should be taken to make sure that indoor air quality (IAQ) problems never occur. The best approach is prevention—which means working diligently to make the right decisions at the right time with respect to the physical environment, both indoor and outdoor, and to create the best possible conditions for teaching and learning.

SITE CONCERNS

Many of the early critical decisions involve site selection. Site-related factors don't just influence the quality of the outdoor environment; they also have a direct effect on the indoor environment.

The selected building site should be appropriate for a high school. An ideal site is rarely available, but a few timely decisions about potential sites can go a long way toward preventing IAQ problems. The terrain, or topography, of the site should be suitable for building economically without the need for major excavation (including rock excavation) or fill; this kind of site is often called a "balanced site." The site must be zoned appropriately, and adjacent land uses need to be considered: for instance, an industrial zone, with its traffic, noise, air quality issues, and other potentially hazardous conditions, would not be well suited for a high school. The underlying soils must be able to support a building and must be free of underground water problems that cannot be economically mitigated. (Underslab drainage systems, particularly if mechanical pumping is necessary, are subject to failure, which could lead to water problems in the slab level of a building.)

If the site contains wetland areas or other watercourses, special permitting from regulatory agencies (e.g., state and local environmental protection agencies, conservation commissions, etc.) is generally required. Wetlands and watercourses may also present problems because of the potential for flooding and the need for insect and other pest control.

The previous uses of the site have to be considered. Schools built on abandoned landfills have sometimes later suffered from elevated levels of pollutants. The site should not be on or near any hazardous waste sites or areas where hazardous material spills or accidents have occurred, because of possible contamination of the underground water supply.

Noisy sites such as industrial areas or areas adjacent to airports should be avoided. Although noise problems can be mitigated by construction detailing, this may involve considerable expense. There should not be any high-voltage power lines on or near the site because of concerns over electromagnetic fields. Nor should there be any natural gas or petrochemical lines on or near the site. Locating near major highways or intersections is also problematic because of elevated automobile emissions levels in the ambient air. All these factors represent potential problem sources that can degrade environmental quality and must be carefully considered and avoided if possible, or mitigated if unavoidable.

Once we have found a site that is acceptable in terms of its preexisting conditions, we need to look at the factors that will be imposed on the site by the new building. Let's take these issues one at a time, beginning (literally) from the ground up. The underlying soils should be able to support the structure without raising concerns about building settlement or having to install unusual and expensive foundation systems. The site should also be able to support any new or existing infrastructure serving the building. Utility services—electrical power, communications cables, water, and sewerage—may need to be brought into the site or, in some cases, may have to be independent, on-site facilities. For example, some sites might require on-site sewage disposal using a conventional septic system or a package sewage treatment plant; ventilation requirements and orientation to prevailing winds may dictate location of such a facility on the site.

Water sources can vary from site to site: some sites have access to the municipal water system; others may require an on-site well or detention basins. At some sites, it may make sense to conserve water by installing an environmentally sensitive gray water system, which recycles some of the building's wastewater.

Other site-related issues might include the need to institute an integrated pest-management plan because of surrounding natural habitats and land-scaped areas; such a plan would control and limit the use of pesticides and herbicides, which could find their way into the building through the ventilation system or open windows or by being tracked in on people's shoes. Stormwater runoff must be controlled for all paved and other impervious surfaces and measured for impact on adjacent sites. And high school sites usually require irrigation for athletic fields and landscaped areas.

BUILDING DESIGN

As the design of the building begins to develop, a multitude of decisions must be made, and most of these decisions will have an impact on the building environment either directly or indirectly. The design of a building is a phased process, beginning with the conceptual, or schematic, design (in which the basic plan of the building and surrounding areas is established); design development (which defines the various systems used in the project); and the creation of construction documents, or working drawings (which contain a level of detail enabling contractors to bid and build the project). In each of these phases decisions are made that will impact the environmental quality of the final design.

Conceptual/Schematic Design. After the building space program has been established, conceptual/schematic design begins. During this phase of design, alternatives are evaluated and initial decisions are made about the form of the building and the basic systems. The organization of the various programmatic elements of the building is analyzed with respect to circulation patterns, adjacency and hierarchy of the spaces, size of spaces, and services in and out of the building. The building program begins to take a physical shape. Basic issues such as orientation to the sun at various times of year and prevailing climatic conditions are considered. Daylighting, insulation, solar heat gain, wind pressure, entrance locations, and roof shapes all can have an effect on the indoor conditions, and so these decisions can have significant impact on the indoor environment.

Logical entrance and egress points are located. The best locations for areas where vehicle exhaust can cause problems—bus loading zones, service areas, loading docks, and waste collection areas—are determined to ensure convenient access, appropriate shielding from view, and appropriate distance from air intakes and operable windows to prevent infiltration of exhaust fumes or offensive odors.

It is during this phase of design that the large volumes of the building are organized. The gymnasium, auditorium, media center, and cafeteria are located to provide convenient access to the public as well as members of the school community. To address air quality concerns, the locker/shower rooms of the physical education suite should be kept well away from the food service and dining areas. Kitchen areas should be located along exterior walls for easy access and proper ventilation. Classroom wings, which are occupied most of the day, are located so that classrooms have access to natural light and ventilation. It is best to isolate noise-generating areas, such as music suites, from the quiet areas such as the media center or counseling areas. Toilet rooms should be readily accessible and have significant negative relative air pressure to ensure that the air flows into them, and this air should be separately exhausted. Public spaces, such as corridors and other assembly spaces, should be adequately sized to avoid overcrowded conditions and help prevent conflict. These programmatic layouts determine the circulation patterns within the building, which, in turn, directly affect noise levels and therefore the quality of the environment and users' perceptions of the building.

Also at this stage, various mechanical systems are evaluated. Conventional systems are compared to more progressive solutions. Centralized ventilation is compared to unit ventilators, and the effect of full air conditioning on these systems is determined. Specialized ventilation is considered for certain areas of the building—science labs, art rooms, workshop areas, food preparation areas, etc.—and separate, dedicated ventilation systems are considered for auditoriums, gymnasiums, and other large assembly spaces to provide adequate ventilation at various levels of occupancy. Designers might also consider the possibility of incorporating any of a number of environmentally friendly systems into the project: for example, a geothermal heating/cooling system; "passive" solar energy collectors (photovoltaics); or fuel-cell technology.

Design Development. During this phase, the approved schematic design is further developed. Wall, floor, and roof systems are more precisely defined, as are mechanical, electrical, communications, and life-safety systems. Here are some of the tasks performed during design development:

- Wall, ceiling and floor systems are detailed to ensure that the correct air-pressure balance is achieved between occupied and interstitial spaces. Occupied spaces should have slight positive pressure to keep the air moving into and through the cavities rather than flowing into the room from the interstitial spaces, which may become contaminated with dust or molds.

- Wall thicknesses and ceiling heights are determined to accommodate the structural and utility systems, and the places where thermal and acoustical insulation will be needed are identified.

- The acoustics of the auditorium, music rooms, and other noise-generating spaces are considered, both in terms of sound quality within these spaces and acoustical isolation from adjacent spaces. Throughout the building, noise levels are controlled by the appropriate use of acoustical materials, proper selection and balancing of mechanical equipment, and choice of furnishings and equipment.

- Exterior walls are designed to accommodate the building structure as well as to maintain thermal properties and weathertightness.

- Doors and windows are located, and the types and sizes of windows are selected. Different kinds of windows—single- or double-hung, casement, fixed units, projecting—have different characteristics and ventilation properties. Window glazing is "custom-tuned" to the orientation of the sun by using special coatings to control UV and heat radiation. Uncontrolled glare can be very distracting, and solar gain from direct sunlight can cause a classroom to overheat and therefore must be ameliorated with appropriate HVAC controls.

- Roof/ceiling and floor/ceiling systems must be designed with IAQ in mind. Ceiling plenums must not be used to supply air distribution. Piping must be properly insulated to avoid condensation buildup on pipe surfaces. Caution must be exercised when using air conditioning systems in the summer months, since warm, moist air, if trapped in the ceiling plenums, could lead to condensation on the ceiling tiles.

- Various ceiling conditions are analyzed and materials selected on the basis of durability and acoustic properties, reflectivity, and aesthetics.

- Roofing and wall systems (including all windows and doors) are analyzed with respect to their thermal values and coordinated with the HVAC systems for calculating the appropriate equipment sizes and capacities.

- HVAC systems are selected and sized up; ductwork and piping layouts are analyzed and coordinated with other systems that serve the building.

- Strategies for controlling visual clutter are determined by designating appropriate locations for bulletin boards, display cases, and other presentation areas.

- Lighting levels are analyzed; lighting layouts are designed; and daylighting opportunities are explored. Increasing natural daylighting not only cuts down on energy usage, it also has the potential to reduce the cooling loads in the building by eliminating some of the heat generated by light fixtures. It has also been shown to be psychologically beneficial.

- The water supply, drainage, fire protection, fire alarm, communications cabling, and intrusion alarm systems are all developed in parallel to ensure proper coordination and fit within the interstitial spaces of the building.

Construction Documents/Working Drawings Phase. Ideally, once design development has been completed, the architect should be able to go ahead and finish the design documents—flushing out the details with information necessary for bidding and building; finalizing engineering systems, site drawings, and architectural specs; and checking all documents for clarity, completeness, and consistency—without any further input from the owner. But we don't live in an ideal world, and so in most cases much remains to be decided through the very end of the project. This should, however, be discouraged to the greatest extent possible, since changes made at this late stage tend to have a ripple effect. (And the later the change, the worse the effect.) For the sake of IAQ, the building committee has the responsibility to ask questions *early* and to ask them *often*—to make sure that the design produced during design development matches expectations as closely as possible.

MATERIAL FINISHES

Finishes can have a dramatic impact on IAQ, and the advantages and disadvantages of using one finish rather than another are often hotly debated. Questions commonly focus on whether to use carpet or alternative flooring materials, acoustic ceiling tile or hard ceilings, and roll-type wall coverings or paint.

School buildings have an extraordinarily high density of occupancy and so must be able to withstand a high level of wear and tear. In the high school setting, the need for durability is paramount, and materials are selected accordingly. Corridors and large assembly areas take the most abuse, and, of course, toilet rooms are often subject to vandalism. It is interesting to note that some of the most durable finishes are also the most inert and least likely to cause indoor air quality problems. For example, terrazzo floors are extremely durable, and, if they are properly installed and are not subjected to any unusual building forces causing them to break up, they do not contribute any pollutants to the indoor air. Similarly durable and inert are concrete block, structural glazed tile used for facing walls, and plaster ceilings. Though these materials are not appropriate for all surfaces in a school building, they should certainly be considered for high-traffic areas.

Moisture problems—which are often implicated in poor IAQ—can result from water being tracked into the building on people's shoes and clothing, problems with high humidity, spills of liquids, and plumbing and building envelope leaks. Absorbent materials such as carpet should not be used on floors in areas where moisture is tracked in from the outside or where liquid spills are frequent. Vinyl wall coverings (VWCs) should be avoided on exterior walls, especially in buildings where air conditioning is heavily used. The vinyl membrane forms a vapor barrier on the inside face of the wall, and moisture condenses between the VWC and underlying paper-faced gypsum wallboard—a condition conducive to mold and fungus growth. Wet rooms, such as toilet rooms and janitors' closets, should have hard ceilings, as should showers, locker rooms, and training rooms. A general rule of thumb is that a porous material (like acoustical tile) will hold moisture and promote the growth of mold and/or mildew, and that such materials should therefore only be used selectively.

CLIMATE CONTROL

The most important factor in ensuring good indoor air quality is to provide the right amount of fresh air—or, to state it technically, to provide the correct number of air changes per hour per person. (This, of course, presumes good quality outdoor air.) In our ideal high school of the future, adequate levels of fresh outdoor air would be brought into the building both through the mechanical system and via natural ventilation (i.e., opening the windows). These levels would not necessarily be limited to the code minimums, but rather would be based on the *ideal* levels for the specific occupancy of any given area. Stale or contaminated air will be quickly exhausted or purged by mechanical fans initiated by sensors with manual overrides, rather than relying strictly on human intervention.

People like to feel that they have some control over comfort conditions, and classroom temperature should therefore be individually controllable within specified comfort ranges to compensate for changing outside conditions throughout the day. A west-facing classroom might need some heat in the early morning, before classes begin, to take the chill out of the air. As soon as the room is occupied with 20 or so students the temperature quickly rises, and it no longer needs supplemental heat. Later in the day, as the afternoon sun heats the space, the room may need cooling. The HVAC system should also be capable of serving flexible spaces, accommodating the increased volume and occupancy if, for example, two classrooms are joined.

Humidity levels should be maintained at normal comfort levels for the geographic area (in New England, between 40 and 50 percent relative humidity). A rather delicate balance must be maintained, however, between providing adequate comfort and deterring growth of mold and mildew. Though low humidity is effective in deterring mold and mildew growth, it can also cause physical discomfort—dry skin, nosebleeds, sore throats, and eye irritation.

A digital climate control system would take on the larger task of maximizing energy efficiency by controlling conditions in unoccupied spaces.

Large group-assembly spaces (auditoriums, music rooms, cafeteria), like classrooms, are likely to be equipped with demand-controlled ventilation systems to temper operating costs. When the room is occupied and the temperature or CO_2 levels reach preset trigger points on sensors around the space, the ventilation system steps up to bring things back to comfortable levels.

CONSTRUCTION CONTROL

Construction control is of vital importance. During construction, areas that may be enclosed and hidden when the building is finished can be contaminated with moisture or other pollutants, and the effects may not appear for months or years after the completion of construction—by which time contractors' warranties will have long since expired. If, for example, a large roofing installation job is not properly sealed up at the end of a workday and it rains overnight, water may infiltrate wall systems but may go undetected by a roofing inspector. The roofing continues, and the wall—containing wet insulation—gets sealed up. Or, to take another example, construction debris or trash might get sealed into ventilation ducts. In either case, it may take a long time for the resulting mold, mildew, or fungus to become apparent, but by that time the building is occupied. The need for a resident engineer or clerk of the works to oversee the quality of workmanship cannot be over-stressed.

COMMISSIONING

Before the building is occupied, there should be a startup period during which all systems are tested for proper functioning. This process is called building *commissioning*. In the commissioning process, which is typically performed by a third party, each system is tested against its design criteria to ensure that the entire facility functions as intended. Corrections and adjustments are made to make sure, prior to occupancy, that the building is safe and healthy. But commissioning should actually go further than this, extending into the post-occupancy period, to ensure that the building functions excellently under conditions of use.

OPERATION AND MAINTENANCE

A new high school for, say, 1,200 students might be as large as 275,000 square feet—an area equivalent to 6.3 acres—and that's just the building. The surrounding lawns and athletic fields must also be maintained. This adds up to a lot of area to sweep, vacuum, polish, and otherwise keep clean on a regular basis. There is little time for the custodial staff to properly clean up incidental moisture-related problems, yet these are precisely the kinds of problems that lead to poor IAQ.

The roof area of such a building might be roughly 183,000 square feet. This is a large area to cover with roofing materials, and, unfortunately, it is unrealistic to expect perfection with any roofing system. In time, leaks will occur. And the thousands of linear feet of piping and hundreds of joints—

subjected to the constant movement of the building described above—are also likely to spring occasional leaks, no matter how well installed. Leaks must be addressed quickly and effectively, since water damage to insulation, wallboard, carpet, wood paneling or flooring, or acoustical ceiling tiles can promote the growth of microorganisms.

Facility maintenance staff should be adequately trained to service and maintain the building systems to keep them running at optimal levels. They should be trained in the techniques proper for cleaning specific materials, and the use of chemical cleaners should be minimized. This way, the staff will become the operatives of an indoor air quality team, recognizing potential indoor air problems and eliminating them before they become hazardous. Besides facility maintenance staff, the overall IAQ team should include representatives of the teachers' organization and parents' group, local administrative staff, nursing office staff, administration staff, and the local health official. The team will be educated about the causes and effects of indoor air quality problems and the methods for resolving the problems quickly when they first occur and are most easily managed. And the team will also be trained in emergency protocols if unsafe conditions arise.

SETTING STANDARDS FOR THE FUTURE

The up-front costs of a high school construction project are enormous, and controlling those costs is usually of great concern. Buildings are designed in ways that contain costs and enable the project to be completed within a restricted budget—and appropriately so. We look to building codes as representing the minimum standard to which we must design, but, too often, anything beyond the basic building code is seen as expendable.

Historically, the primary intent of building codes has not been to establish design criteria but rather to protect the life of the public. In recent years, however, national codes have been revised to include energy standards, and, by doing so, regulators have extended the codes' purpose beyond the primary intent of protecting life. Inclusion of these energy codes serves the public good by incorporating requirements for energy conservation that benefit everyone. This extension of the codes bodes well for indoor air quality. Setting minimum standards for indoor air quality would benefit everyone both directly, through exposure to a cleaner, healthier environment, and indirectly, through generally reduced health care costs and less time lost from work because of illness.

Building code commissions have recognized the need for setting standards for indoor air quality but have relied on other organizations to lead the way. For example, the American Society of Heating, Refrigeration and Air Conditioning Engineers (ASHRAE) established the nationally recognized standard for air-exchange rates based on specific occupancies. These standards are referenced in the codes and have generally been effective, but, again, it must be recognized that these represent *minimum* standards for comfort. The federal Occupational Safety and Health Administration (OSHA) establishes maximum recommended exposure levels for a long list of chemicals and compounds, but these standards are for the adult working environment and are not necessarily applicable to students of various ages and stages of physical development. Building product manufacturers, driven by competition to provide the best products, have to a certain extent been self-regulating, but one must remember that those same competitive forces drive down manufacturing costs and hence tend to keep products at a minimum level of acceptability. Competitive forces tend to keep products at a minimum standard of acceptance. These trends, taken together, have resulted in minimum "guideline standards" for indoor air quality.

For the high school of the future we must set a higher goal, a higher standard for design. The goal should be to create the *optimal* environment for the educational process—one that provides all users with a clean, safe, and healthy environment. That environment should be free of the distractions of a fault-ridden building and should ensure comfort levels that allow students to perform at their highest levels. Such a design gives the community a reliable and long-lasting facility—a monument to civic pride and a testimony to the community's willingness to invest in its children's future.

Chapter 12

Exceptional Kids Need More Feet: Designing Barrier-Free Schools for Special Education Students

At Trumbull High School in the Bridgeport suburb of Trumbull, Connecticut, the Planning and Placement Team applauded junior Shane Spencer's involvement with the audiovisual club and developed an Individual Educational Plan (IEP) for him that called for AV club participation before and after school. Shane's father and mother, who were deeply involved with development of the plan, pointed out that, although the concept was fine, it wouldn't work because Shane, a student with multiple disabilities who is confined to a wheelchair, could not open the school's front door.

After lengthy discussion with the Trumbull Board of Education, it was determined that an electronic door opener costing $2,400 would solve the problem. An agreement, in keeping with the IEP, was reached in which the Board of Ed would install the opener, paying for the device and associated construction costs out of emergency/contingency facility funding.

During the same period, the Trumbull district determined that it needed an alternate education facility for approximately 50 high school students, some identified as special education students and many with emotional and related behavior problems. The district decided that this facility should be configured into existing middle school space. The facility was designed with IEP requirements in mind, and a substantial effort was made to accommodate different students' varying needs. Costs associated with this renovation added up to approximately $200,000.

Another Connecticut high school, this one in the Hartford suburb of Plainville, currently faces an uncomfortable dilemma. In response to a recent state ruling declaring that playing-field press boxes must be fully accessible, school officials have shut down their football field's press box—part of a structure built long before disabled-access legislation was ever introduced—as they search for an affordable and workable solution. At this writing, the Plainville High School administration is investigating the possibility of installing a lift—having already decided that constructing a wheelchair ramp would be infeasible or prohibitively expensive. Meanwhile, the old press box goes unused.

EDUCATIONAL ENTITLEMENTS AND SCHOOL ARCHITECTURE

School districts across the country are facing extraordinary demands on their facilities. The reasons for the seemingly inexorable increases in space needs are many—including, for example, rocketing enrollments, the expansion of community recreational programs, and curriculum development that focuses on providing space for collaboration, hands-on activities, and a problem-solving approach to learning. But one of the prime movers pushing up space requirements is the expansion of educational entitlements due children with disabilities resulting from the Individuals with Disabilities Education Act (IDEA) of 1990. That federal law, combined with the Americans with Disabilities Act (ADA) of 1990 and with state laws and local mandates, has created a situation in which schools' legal and moral obligations to attend to the needs of special education students sometimes conflict with districts' facility and financial resources. Much of the space and money crunch happens a the high school level, but the problems certainly aren't limited to high schools. IDEA extended protections and entitlements to children younger than five years of age, which means that many school districts are wrestling with questions about how to provide barrier-free access to educational opportunity from the earliest preschool years through 12th grade.

School officials are hardly unaware of these developments—or of the space and financial quandaries they so often raise. Yet, to our knowledge, there has been no comprehensive study of the impact that disabilities/special education legislation and case law has had on school districts nationally. Although there have been numerous attempts to study the problem and many special hearings on the topic before national, state, and local legislative bodies, supportive data falls short of being comprehensive. It is just too difficult to uncover all the expenditures or to discern their rationales—or, in fact, to determine with any precision the relationships between particular expenditures and the special-education needs that instigated them. For instance, what indicator, other than a transcript of the Board of Ed discussion itself, could possibly lead to uncovering the Trumbull electronic door-opener expenditure? The actual expense was buried in an emergency facility fund. There is a paucity of information about the strategies that districts pursue to make sure that the architectural design of new and renovated schools meets special education and related space needs. If such information were systematically compiled, it might help districts contain costs related to special education, now and in the long run.

In the absence of a national or systematic study, we can offer only anecdotal evidence of the kinds of challenges school districts are facing. But that evidence is, we believe, telling, and it has led us to speculate on the architectural ramifications of special education entitlements. What follows is a discussion of these implications, with an eye toward helping school officials prepare to work with architects to ensure that special education needs are met. Of course, the financial pinch that school districts feel is partly created by the fact that state reimbursements have not caught up with the increased square-footage demands arising from special education entitlements and other factors. Legislative action on this score is, unfortunately, likely to be long in coming. In the meantime, school officials need concrete advice on how to best serve all of a district's students while keeping special education-related costs as low as possible. As we'll indicate, this is a very tall order indeed.

SPECIFIC SPACE IMPLICATIONS

In the decade since ADA and IDEA were signed into law, Americans (architects included) have learned quite a lot about how to accommodate people with physical disabilities and to ensure their easy access to all sorts of facilities. We have a fair amount of experience and now deal reasonably well with access issues involving elevators, entranceways (including the provision of ramps and interior automatic doors), lavatories, and so on. We still have a long way to go, however.

As a society, we haven't yet come to grips with some of the subtler aspects of disabilities legislation, which aims at ensuring that disabled people participate equally in all the opportunities that we provide to the able-bodied. In schools, this means making sure that, to the greatest degree possible, physically disabled students are able to enjoy access to all parts of the curriculum as well as all extracurricular activities. For instance, we can no longer relegate student clubs or groups, like the yearbook editorial team, to constricted, inaccessible, out-of-the-way offices or storage rooms. If a wheelchair-bound student wants to serve as a manager of the football or field hockey team, architecture and landscaping must serve his or her wishes: locker rooms must be fully accessible, as must playing fields and, as we saw above, auxiliary facilities as press boxes.

So far, this seems simple enough in concept, and the space (and cost) implications might seem relatively clear. In actuality, they can be exceedingly complex. To take just a few examples: When designing new school gymnasiums or rehabbing old ones, architects must take pains to ensure that bleachers are accessible, which might involve the addition of ramps, the implementation of new handhold standards, and the like. Such measures aren't only expensive, they also have an impact on space. (In a renovated gym, the number of seats might be reduced by as much as 20 percent to permit these kinds of changes.) Making a school's pool accessible might involve the installation of an electric lift to lower physically disabled students into the water. Here again, there isn't just a cost impact (the expense of the equipment) but a space impact as well. The poolside areas must be larger or differently configured in order to accommodate the apparatus.

The list of architectural interventions necessary to accommodate physically disabled students has grown quiet long—and the impact on space and budget is burgeoning accordingly. In auditorium design, for example, it's no longer satisfactory to designate a certain seating area for wheelchairs; such spaces should be scattered around the house, so that wheelchair-bound students—like all others—have a choice of vantage. Lifts must be provided to enable disabled students to access the pit and the control room.

The design of band and choral-group practice rooms must likewise be reconceived: the old tiered arrangement turns out to be impractical for disabled-access purposes in most school buildings, since wheelchair ramps capable of servicing all the tiers are expensive—and require that the room be enormous, since the angle at which such ramps can incline is very slight. (Flat-floored band rooms eliminate the access problem but create difficulties with sightlines and acoustics for which solutions must be found.)

Hallway design must factor in a host of variables relating to access: For instance, wheelchair-accessible water fountains typically protrude fairly far into corridors and may necessitate increasing corridor width. (And, for school buildings, such fountains and their mountings must be extra strong, since athletically inclined students tend to use them as ad hoc pommel horses!) Corridors must incorporate buzzer-equipped "refuge" spaces to which wheelchair bound students can retreat when having difficulties or in case of fire. To aid visually impaired students, all hallway signage must include Braille versions, and doors to off-limits rooms must have knurled knobs to warn against entering those areas. And lab design, too, must accommodate students with disabilities—including the provision of special-height counters for students with wheelchairs.

It's also important to point out that "barriers" don't just consist of the physical impediments—walls, stairs, doors—restricting disabled students' movement. A "barrier" can involve what is not there as much as what is. For example, not only do some assistive devices (e.g. wheelchairs) require space, but many electronic assistive devices require recharging stations; and space for these is not usually anticipated in a school's design. A barrier limiting a physically disabled child's equal access to educational opportunity is thereby being erected "by omission," one might say.

PLANNING AND PLACEMENT TEAM FACILITIES

Most facility modifications are drawn from decisions taken by the federally mandated Planning and Placement Teams that exist in all public schools across the nation. These teams make decisions based on what they think is realistically possible. If, for example, a child is having a bad allergic reaction in a classroom, the PPT plan might call for installation of an air purifier and/ or removal of a suspect rug. The use of whiteboards instead of blackboards has to some extent been driven by dust-related disability complications.

It's obvious that Planning and Placement Teams need somewhere to meet. What may not be so obvious is that a well-functioning PPT meeting space has some relatively complex programmatic requirements.

First, the main PPT conference room must be fairly large. It isn't uncommon for a PPT meeting to include the following people: the student, his or her parents, as many as five teachers, a social worker, a guidance counselor, one or more representatives from the school district, one or two attorneys for the Board of Education, one or two attorneys or other advisors representing the student, a stenographer, and possibly a state appointed mediator. That list of participants, as long as it is, is not necessarily complete. This means we are talking about a conference room capable of comfortably accommodating upwards of 20 people. PPT negotiations resemble other legal procedures in which, for example, parties may at certain points wish to retire from the negotiations in order to consider offers, discuss strategy, and so on. Therefore, it may be advisable for the PPT space to be configured as a suite that includes a main conference room and one or more auxiliary "caucus" rooms where the parties can sequester themselves, if necessary.

PPT spaces also need to be private and, to ensure that recording equipment works properly, insulated against outside noise. They need to be air conditioned as well, since many PPT meetings occur during the summer months, before the beginning of the school year. (A given hearing may last for several days, which makes the need to air condition PPT spaces even more urgent.) These combinations of requirements of size, privacy, quiet, and air conditioning mean that it is often wise to make the PPT meeting spaces *dedicated* meeting spaces. Needless to say, setting aside an area of a school building specifically for this purpose can have a significant impact on overall square footage.

"SPECIAL EDUCATION": EXPANDING THE DEFINITION

In some ways, "Special Education," traditionally understood as applying to students with physical disabilities and/or diagnosable learning disabilities, may be too narrow and limiting a term to designate contemporary school districts' efforts to ensure equal educational opportunity for all students. Perhaps we ought instead to speak of "alternate" education," a term that would cover not only the legally mandated special education strategies that are designed to assist children with physical and/or learning disabilities but also those strategies that districts are pursuing to ensure that students with family, emotional, or psychological problems also receive the fullest, best educational experience possible. (Many of these students are considered "pre-special education.")

To help students in this latter group, (and to reduce the chance that students with emotional problems will disrupt other students' learning process), many schools today are employing techniques to help students manage their anger, and even to mediate disputes that arise among students at large, with the aim of preventing disagreements from escalating into more serious problems. These strategies, too, have a very real effects on space needs and on how space is allocated. For example, whether a school relies on trained student mediators or a salaried anger-management/mediation specialist, rooms must be set aside for this purpose.

As we make progress in learning how to deal with wall, stair, and door barriers, technology is giving us the ability to deal with barriers of a different nature. When students cannot, for some legitimate reason, leave their homes to come to school, schools have traditionally sent tutors to provide at-home instruction. In a technologically enhanced educational environment, however, schools will in all probability be required to telecommunicate lessons in full-motion audio/video format utilizing the Internet or an intranet system. Likewise, computer technology provides in-school solutions for students who have problems hearing, seeing, and/or writing. Students with these kinds of difficulties can be assisted by district-owned laptops with earphones, large-print capabilities, and/or voice-recognition software.

The goal, of course, is inclusiveness: to make sure, whenever and wherever possible, that special-needs students are not segregated but have the opportunity and ability to learn, eat, play, study, and travel to and from campus with so-called "regular" students. The infrastructure necessary to support the new technology includes room for sophisticated wiring and switching gear, repair/maintenance space, production areas, training stations, and simple charging and disbursement stations. And these specialized space needs translate into extraordinary expense.

"SOFT" COSTS AND INFLATIONARY FACTORS

To appreciate the full impact on design and construction costs of accommodating special-needs students in all areas of academic life, one must also figure in the nearly unavoidable increases in "soft" costs that such efforts entail. For example, school-facility planning costs are proportionally higher than in the past: as case law and state regulatory decisions continue to mount, architects and planners have come to anticipate that a significant amount of redrawing will usually be necessary following state review of plans.

For a variety of reasons ranging from construction industry labor and building-material shortages to the decreasing availability of suitable sites for building new schools (and concomitant increases in the need to perform extensive site remediation before construction begins), inflation rates in school construction are already higher than the average across-the-board rates calculated by the Consumer Price Index. Accommodating students with disabilities exacerbates this inflationary trend because of the rise in the number of code-mandated requirements that must be incorporated into facility design and followed during construction.

Moreover, incorporating features that enhance access for students with disabilities inevitably widens the gap between gross and net square feet. School officials are sometimes puzzled by this, since the gross-to-net ratio can grow even when stringent efforts are made to limit a school facility's size—for instance, by reducing classroom dimensions. But there's really no mystery: many of the disabled-access and related elements mentioned above—wider corridors, hallway refuge spaces, recharging stations, rooms for air-conditioning equipment, and so on—have the effect of increasing gross square footage disproportionately.

AGREEMENT, KNOWLEDGE, PATIENCE, AND UNDERSTANDING

In the face of these stepped-up demands on school facilities, what can a school administration do to stem the tide of rising costs related to meeting exceptional student needs? The answer to the question is not abundantly clear, but some school districts have successfully implemented an administrative approach that emphasizes agreement among officials, sound knowledge and expert counsel, patience, and a willingness to understand parents' concerns. Below, we describe this approach—one that, in broad terms, could be adopted by any school district.

Educators are ethically and professionally charged with the task of doing what is right to meet students' needs and help them to learn. On this basis, one might suggest that an administrator will always be on solid ground if he or she advocates paying the bill—no matter how high—for any apparently valid special needs request.

The problem is that some of the requests come with enormous price tags. For instance, supporting a residential placement for an emotionally disturbed student might require an annual expenditure on the part of the district of, say, $75,000. This, of course, would correspondingly reduce the amount of money available for other important educational projects. Knowing this, most administrators will try to hold off on making a large special-education expenditure even where such an expenditure will be a step toward meeting an exceptional student's needs.

But, to contain special education-related expenditures successfully, the superintendent, the administrator in charge of special education, and the district's business manager must be in agreement about which requests to support, which to oppose, and where to draw the line. If a special education director takes an issue that has not been agreed upon to the board of education, a state mediator, and/or the Exceptional Children's Parents Organization, the director is likely to win the argument and the town to be forced to spend the money. The three administrators must therefore learn how to work together and to present a unified front.

In many cases, even when a school district administration presents a solid position opposing a parent's request, the parent will call for a hearing with the state's department of education or will go to court—and stands a good chance of winning favorable decision. The board of education and district administration must therefore have the assistance of an adept and knowledgeable lawyer with experience in the special education field and knowledge of how the school administration, board of education members, state mediators, and the courts would be likely to react if pressed on a given issue. In preparing to deal with special education requests, districts have to be ready to "pay the price" by having a knowledgeable lawyer on staff, backed by a quality law firm on retainer.

Taking problems into the legal arena is not always prudent or wise, however. Understanding how a particular request accords with legal requirements and understanding something about the particular parent or parents making the request—being able to guess with some degree of certainty the kind of action they might take if the request is denied—are essential. For one thing, administrators must know when to "fold their cards" and grant a request. In many cases a partial solution to the problem may be acceptable enough that the district can delay having to lay out the comparatively huge amount of money that meeting the full request would require. And sometimes parents' concerns can be assuaged by less costly solutions—assigning a teacher's aid to provide tutoring, for example, or purchasing a laptop with special features designed to ease the student's learning difficulties. Getting all the parties to agree to accept an arbitrator's decision may be helpful in resolving some situations.

In all cases, human relations skills are absolutely necessary when dealing with parents who often feel that they are their children's only advocates. The administration must exhibit patience and understanding. Many an advocate for exceptional children has been stonewalled by school administrators only to rebound and to win the argument with a resolution that is significantly more costly than the initial request. It always pays to bend over backwards to support special education students, their parents, and their advocates in booster groups and parent/teacher associations. Making a real effort to understand the challenges that students with disabilities face goes a long way toward bridging communication gaps. The record is full of cases where what appeared to be a minority position turned out to have majority support. In the 1999/2000 school year, again in Trumbull, Connecticut, the district administration and eventually the Board of Education agreed to fight for a nineteen-year-old, mentally retarded high school senior named David. David wanted to swim on the varsity team, but Connecticut Inter-Scholastic Association Conference ruled him ineligible because he was nineteen. Athletic directors and principals across the state joined hands to fight the Trumbull position, arguing that it would not be wise to let David swim.

David's articulate, dedicated parents were prepared to fight the school district and the state all by themselves. But, sensing the district's compassion, they persuaded the district to battle the state's athletic bureaucracy. The Trumbull lawyer and his supportive law firm took the case on pro bono, and Trumbull won in the local court and on appeal in the

United States circuit court. The district was prepared to proceed all the way to the U.S. Supreme Court when the state athletic association realized it was backing a loosing cause and withdrew. Press coverage of the case cast a favorable light on the Trumbull School District and strengthened the administration's hand in dealing with other special education matters.
In general, parents of special-needs students are well aware that school districts have limited funding. They just want to be assured that districts are doing as much as they can to support their children. With patience and knowledge, a middle ground can usually be reached. Administrators who are prepared to suggest a range of alternatives and are willing to negotiate— and who are aided by an expert, capable lawyer—will be the most successful at controlling costs while satisfying concerned parents.

In this climate, where demands on school facilities constantly change and inexorably increase, it is incumbent on architects to become as knowledgeable as possible about all the issues affecting school design, to stay abreast of regulatory changes, and to keep school officials informed regarding how state and local mandates and case-law decisions will impact design, construction, and associated costs. Most of all, though, architects must counsel patience—and must do their part to help administrators prepare for the long, and occasionally difficult, road ahead, as our society strives to meet its obligations to special-needs students.

Chapter 13

Harmony in Value Engineering
by Marcia T. Palluzzi, LA

At the onset of any building project, all parties seek to create an environment that inspires. Often the process is tempered by practical, fiscal, and/or political challenges. It is during such controversies that value is established and inspiration becomes visible. Value engineering is the manifestation of the balance between priority and constructability.

Value engineering is most successful when it is fully integrated into the design process. It involves more than just changing or removing building materials or program functions. In fact, it involves seeing the path to the finished project in new ways. It is the component that makes the intangible tangible, often by creating a compromise between an idea and an affordable solution. Our beliefs about money and our understanding of the construction process work hand in hand in the value engineering process.

Our beliefs about money, and especially the voters' beliefs as revealed by the referendum process, can dramatically impact the course of the design process. Perceived need and actual need can be two very different things. It is essential that the building committee and board of education, working in conjunction with the architect, craft a financial strategy plan while the schematic building design is under development. Such a plan should include a communications strategy for gaining voter understanding, acceptance, and support of the project. (See Chapter 15, "Passing Your School Referendum," in this book.) It should also include an analysis of state reimbursement potential, a compilation of possible rebates for energy-efficient systems, and an assessment of the current labor market, availability of building materials, and the timing of similar projects in the region.

Oftentimes, value engineering decisions are made early on, during conception of the project. Expenditures on administrative office space, extensive parking areas, and large athletic complexes are frequently eliminated at the start before other cost options are investigated.

The conception period of a project is, in fact, a critical time in the value engineering process. Feasibility studies, often part of the conception process, provide a valuable analysis of potential paths that a project can take. The decisions to rehabilitate, build additions, or construct a completely new facility all have different cost implications. Consideration of facility needs, enrollment projections, state reimbursement, and energy rebates are some specific factors affecting the design.

Judgments related to initial cost versus long-term durability must be determined in the value engineering process. Balancing these two factors and making related decisions requires clear communication about the cost of materials, maintenance, and life-cycle of the products. For example, it is common to use dry wall instead of masonry on interior walls although the use of masonry is probably more cost-effective over the long run. Floor finishes, particularly in the cafeteria and hallways, will stand up longer and be easier to maintain if they are of high quality. The dollars spent to strip and wax low-grade finishes would in many cases probably more than pay for an upgrade.

Such decisions can also significantly impact the health and welfare of the individuals who will occupy the building. Lighting and acoustical treatments significantly impact vision and hearing. Improperly diffused ceiling lights can obscure lighting on computer screens, causing eyestrain or headaches. Improper computer furniture will affect posture, causing neck aches or backaches or even serious repetitive strain injuries. Acoustical treatments in a band room are critical to preventing damage to musicians' eardrums. Another approach to reducing costs involves the re-evaluation of needs. Prioritizing the inclusion of certain spaces or reducing the sizes of critical spaces will bring the costs down. Compromising on the spaces or storage areas within the school can, however, have a large impact on the functioning and management of the facility. Cutting back on space is often the first strategy pursued because it is difficult to quantify the value of additional space. At this point in the space-adjustment process it is extremely important to obtain input from the board of education and knowledgeable educators to understand any related impact on student learning potential.

Lastly, the building systems should come under scrutiny. Heating and ventilation systems improperly distributed, balanced, and filtered will produce an unhealthy building with dirty ducts and/or hot-cold spots. Leaving air conditioning out of portions of a building will affect year-round building usage. But large, expensive facilities should be able to be used throughout the year. Also relevant in a discussion of mechanical systems is the opportunity to save money on operating the building through energy-efficient equipment. Although such equipment is costly, rebates from utility companies are often available.

So when and where do we value engineer a project? Ideally, it begins to occur during the conception of the project and continues from there. It is clearly a collaborative process, which must balance need, funding, and creativity into a harmonious whole. Conscious effort to be aware of the cost estimating and financial strategic plan for the building will forestall surprises during the bidding process. Rather then pulling easily calculated items out of the equation, value engineering must be based on sound planning and design considerations. Time spent to gather data, communicate findings, and discuss priorities will pay off in the long run. Educated, "quality" decisions—made in a collaborative fashion—have the best chance of being cost-effective and providing the best learning environment for the student of tomorrow.

Chapter 14

Technology Utilization: A Futuristic Vision of Technology and Square Feet

Over the past decade, the number of square feet per high school student has been steadily increasing in new high schools across the country. In new high schools, square footage per student often exceeds state standards and becomes nonreimbursable to the municipality. It therefore seems prudent to look at ways in which the square footage of new high schools might be reduced. In the past, new educational technologies typically *added* square footage to schools (for example, by adding space for computer stations to classroom). Now, however, technological advances are giving us the opportunity to bring square footages down, at least in certain program areas.

THE CLASSROOM

In 1999, Fletcher-Thompson, Inc., surveyed superintendents of 40 Connecticut school districts. The educators we interviewed agreed that high school teachers are gradually becoming *facilitators* of learning rather than presenters of information. In the future, teachers will spend more of their time working with students individually, developing and reworking individualized "educational learning prescriptions," than they will spend presenting material to an entire class.

Over the next decade, the school day is likely to remain about the same in terms of when classes begin and end, the division of the day into class periods, and so on, but the *learning year* will be extended, moving toward a year-round, 365-day phenomenon. Students will work on their school-related projects on the beach, in the ski lodge, and while riding planes and trains, as the spirit moves them. Student-teacher interaction will in many cases be by telecommunication. Some information will still be presented, as before, by in-class lecture, but that will be supplemented and, in some cases, replaced by on-line lectures. Discussion of information presented will take place in small groups in school and on-line, as well.

The high school classroom, because of these changes in teaching and learning style, will undergo a transformation. It will in all probability consist of a well-equipped teaching station with a teacher-student-parent conferencing area and a flexible student seating format that allows for work/discussion stations for 25 or more students.

The student work/discussion stations will have room for wireless laptops, some reference material, and comfortable chairs. The laptops will have wireless access to the Internet. Much student communication will be via laptop screen or other electronic reader. There will be no attempt to include space in the classroom for book bags, other peripheral equipment, or other furniture. The laptop bag (with room inside for personal items) will be all that the student will carry.

Everything above can be comfortably fit into a 650 square foot area—approximately 20 percent less space than we see in most classroom design schemes today.

LOCKERS AND HALLWAYS

If each student accesses information via a laptop, personal digital assistant (PDA), or similar wireless device, the need to carry books will be sharply reduced. Lockers for each student can therefore be eliminated and replaced by student storage rooms/coatrooms. As we say above, laptops will be carried home, together with lunch and/or other personal items, in a relatively small bag. As laptops become smaller, the size of the bag will approximate that of a medium-sized briefcase. The book bag will disappear because textbooks and other reading material will be accessed electronically.

In today's high schools, security concerns often focus on corridors containing lockers—a natural place for arguments and disputes to break out. With the elimination of hallway lockers, related surveillance and security issues will be reduced.

Factoring in the elimination of student lockers and the addition of a coatroom we might just be able to reduce hallway size by as much as 20 percent off today's average.

Although it will take time to set up a comprehensive electronic reading system, and while it may pay to wait for readers with better resolution than today's technology permits, it is the right time to design schools to anticipate this change.

THE MEDIA CENTER

New communications technologies are certain to have a very significant impact on the design of media centers in future high schools, but this is one area in which resistance to change is also very great. For example, the widespread adoption of electronic books and the electronic readers used to download and access them will make it possible to reduce the number of book stacks and the space that is now used to house them. Such a thought, however, brings shivers to many librarians—a fear that's akin to that experienced by "tree huggers" in the face of the proverbial chainsaw. Eliminating some stacks is, however, inevitable and will probably start in the reference department. (The superintendents surveyed acknowledged the advent of the electronic reader but predicted that full-scale adoption would be a slow, evolutionary process.)

Despite resistance to this change, we believe it is safe to predict an eventual 50 percent cutback in stack space. As stack space wanes, the number of individual study stations and collaborative conferencing and teleconferencing rooms in media centers will increase, and we think that about half of the space now given over to stacks will be required for new individual workstations and collaborative environments. The net square footage reduction in a typical media center could therefore be as much as 25 percent.

SCIENCE LABS

The ninth and tenth grade science lab is gradually evolving into a one-room, combined presentation and virtual lab space. At those grade levels (at least in some schools), experiments are now being conducted virtually on computer screens, eliminating the need for glassware, special furniture, and lab-counter gas, water, and power sources. It is much easier and more efficient to perform dissections using a popular anatomy software like "ADAM" than on a real animal! These all-purpose science labs for the lower grades do not need prep rooms or separate presentation classrooms. The superintendents we surveyed generally agreed that ninth/tenth grade science labs could be generic, technologically supported classrooms. This change would enable us to reduce a new high school's total science square footage by approximately 20 percent.

Advanced-placement chemistry, biology, and physics courses will, however, continue to require labs in which students can perform real, hands-on experiments (perhaps supplemented by virtual guidance). Well equipped labs—with gas, water, electricity, and associated code/safety items—will therefore remain essential necessities for advanced science courses.

LARGE SCHOOL VERSUS SMALL SCHOOL

Many have argued that students are more likely to be lonely and lost in a large school than in a small one. Though the superintendents we polled for the most part favored smaller high schools—in the 1,000- to 1,200-student range—the preference for smaller schools no longer makes as much sense as it once did. The traditional barriers to communication imposed by walls, distance, and size are becoming progressively less important. The existence of an "intranet community" in each new school will allow students to meet and get to know one another online through a variety of interactive modes.

As communications technologies support interactivity no matter what the size of the school, economics becomes more important as a deciding factor. Large high schools are able to provide a wider variety of program choices because of economies of scale, and, on a per-student basis, they are cheaper to build. A high school for 3,000 students has less square footage than two 1,500-student high schools. And, of course, large high schools can be broken down into "houses," which give students a greater sense of belonging. Therefore, despite continuing resistance to the idea, the large high school seems to make sense for the future.

BUSING AND THE GLOBAL POSITION SATELLITE (GPS) SYSTEM

Assuming that each student's schedule will eventually be individualized, it will be possible to use that schedule to program related arrival and departure times, as well as general school bus transportation needs.

In accommodating individualized schedules, today's 40-bus district might be able to meet the same need by running only 20 buses. This adjustment could be made by operating each bus all day long, rather than only early in the morning and again in the afternoon. The 20 buses could have 10 different district-wide routes and be programmed to give door-to-door service at the most economical time, as dictated by a "chip reservation" system. For instance, the student would input his or her schedule for the day or week, and the transportation system would reserve his or her arrival and departure times. The student's bar-coded personal chip, when read at the bus door, would find the student's dropoff spot on the electronic route. A Global Position Satellite (GPS) system aboard the bus would navigate for the driver. The net result could be an approximately 20 percent reduction in the cost of bus operation, based on the assumption that the first costs of technology to operate such a system might be somewhat substantial and would reduce overall savings achieved by the system.

The system would also provide relief by downsizing pickup and dropoff site development problems. The student would arrive and depart from the high school in accordance with his or her own schedule, leading to a much wider variation in arrival and departure times. It would not be uncommon for a student to arrive at school at 9:00 a.m. and depart at 6:00 p.m., for example, or to arrive at 10:00 a.m. and depart at 2:00 p.m..

Also, with each student wearing a personalized chip, it will be possible for the school community via the GPS system to know where the student is at all times (assuming, of course, that the student is carrying the chip). While this suggestion may seem farfetched at the moment because of the limitations of current technology and the tradition of today's home and school schedules, it should be noted that many of our school buses today leave and arrive filled to less than half their capacity because students are already on individual schedules and arrive and depart by other means. Recognizing existing travel patterns and being able to stagger schedules—with cooperation from staff, parents, and students—could result in a sharp discount in transportation services provided, even without involving a chip or a GPS system.

PHYSICAL EDUCATION

Unfortunately, we have not found ways in which technology will allow us to condense physical education space and/or schedules. In fact, one could easily make the argument that the future high school's physical education components should be *increased* in size. It is possible, however, that with sophisticated scheduling, the use of improved artificial turf, and the application of the inflatable roof and/or multi-purpose fieldhouse/superdome structure, phys ed facilities can be designed and built to accommodate multiple uses in a weatherproof and more cost-effective environment. It is clear that a large high school project has a better chance of including such a facility than does any other municipal project.

Such a facility—called a "hard dome"—is under consideration in Rye Brook, New York.

This 120,000 square foot sports dome, to be constructed on vacant land at Port Chester Middle School, would house a two-level golf driving range and offer miniature golf, basketball courts, and convertible fields for baseball, soccer, football, and softball. The plan also calls for a track, lockers, volleyball court, food court, fitness center, video arcade, and computer training lab. The structure would stand 65 feet high at its summit. Parking would accommodate 280 vehicles, with an extra 30-vehicle gate-controlled lot for use by the school district.

It may also be possible to individualize physical education instruction by giving credit for out-of-school activities such as participation on a soccer team or following an exercise program at home. Clearly, physical education can be acquired after or before regular school hours, but any facility savings achieved by such scheduling would probably be offset by increased facility demand by a wide variety of groups.

Last but not least, we have to ask, "Do we really need all that shower square footage?" Girls' showers, particularly, are rarely used. Reducing the square footage now given over to showers will, in many cases, necessitate legislative action to change state regulations, but this is certainly something that should be seriously considered.

FINE ARTS AND THE AUDITORIUM

Like phys ed, the arts are likely to require more, not less, space in the future high school. Student involvement in the arts is growing, and the performing arts are viewed as increasingly important, both for the school population and for the wider community. Practice room and rehearsal space as well as space to store instruments and house audio/visual equipment are showing up in more and more building specifications. (Spaces for live practice and performance seem to serve as an antidote to the anonymity associated with Internet interaction and virtual "experience.")

Communities are asking for high school auditoriums with large seating capacities so that everyone can gather to appreciate, celebrate, and debate. While a square footage cutback is hard to recommend here, combined town/school use can make more efficient use of fine arts and auditorium space.

PRACTICAL ARTS (INDUSTRIAL ARTS, UNIFIED ARTS, AND/OR TECHNOLOGY)

As in some parts of the science curriculum, some instruction in the practical arts lends itself to computer-based instruction and the virtual-experience mode of learning. But hands-on experience remains a necessity. One has to assume that to be able to saw, drill, and use a tape measure will always be important. To fix a leaky faucet, wire a plug, and change a flat tire are skills that will also be with us quite a while. Once again, it is hard to envision square footage reductions in practical arts; in fact, more space may be needed as computer repair training at the high school level becomes more and more commonplace.

CONFERENCING SPACE

It is a rare high school today that has adequate administration space. Because conferencing is at the very heart of the administrative process, enough space should be available that administrators, counselors, nurses, recruiters, planning and placement teams (PPTs), students, parents, and visiting officials can do their work efficiently, collaboratively, and well. Such space should be equipped with teleconferencing capability.

As the teacher becomes more of a counselor, the need for the traditional sort of interaction between students and counselors diminishes—*but* that will be offset by an increasing need for one-on-one interaction between students and their teacher/counselors. The traditional counselor will spend more time training the teacher to counsel the student.

With the advent of counseling related to students' genetic capacities and the dispensing of designer drugs, the nurse's office will, we think, expand into a nurse/doctor space with room for conferencing and probably for drug prescribing and distributing.

The superintendents we polled agreed that increases are needed in the space allocated for nurses, counselors, and administrators. They also stressed the need for more conference room.

Students, of course, need conferencing space, too. If a school has conflict resolution, anger mitigation, or personal problem-solving programs, conferencing space must be allocated for these purposes. And the movement to help young people learn about and use democratic principles through collaborative learning is likewise influencing high schools' architectural requirements. The higher-order thinking program called "HOT"—a good example of a democratic learning program—calls for large spaces for assembly and smaller conferencing and communication opportunities. (This program is usually supported by sophisticated electronic communication systems.) And student government organizations also need space that allows for large group discussion and voting.

Given all these factors, the high school of the future probably needs a 20 percent increase in square footage for conferencing and related office space.

REDUCING OVERALL SQUARE FOOTAGE BY 20 PERCENT

Our algebraic summary of square foot additions and deductions indicates that we have not quite achieved a 20 percent across-the-board reduction in the square footage of tomorrow's high school. To reach that overall 20 percent reduction we offer distance-learning efficiency as a further potential reduction catalyst. Asynchronous distance learning performed by keyboard and/or voice recognition is useful for individualized instruction. Synchronous/interactive full-motion audio/video distance learning is good for presentations and discussion. The synchronous mode works best in states where yearly calendar and daily schedules are similar across districts, allowing for similar class schedules.

If we assume that today's high school is currently planned for 85 percent room utilization efficiency, proper use of both kinds of distance learning should be able to increase the room utilization rate to approximately 90 percent. Small classes in different high schools can, using this technique, be merged into normal class sizes, thereby reducing operational costs and the associated number of classrooms needed.

We think that distance learning used on a relatively wide scale will balance our proposed square footage additions and thereby allow us to envision a high school in the foreseeable future with an overall 20 percent square footage reduction.

Consequently, if a new high school today costs on the order of $50 million, the cost of our high school of tomorrow, based on noninflated dollars and a 20 percent square footage reduction, would be significantly less. Operational costs could be reduced in a similar fashion.

EDITORIAL SUGGESTION (TONGUE IN CHEEK)

Educators are good at spending saved money, and in most cases their actions result in value added to the learning experience. So we suggest that the 20 percent savings be split with the taxpayer, with the net result being that the high school of the foreseeable future could wind up adding value to the learning experience *and* costing the taxpayer less.

Perhaps 50 percent of the square footage cutback savings should be designated to pay for the technology necessary to make the savings happen, assuming that most of the new technology would also provide for value added education. This, we think, would make for a "win-win" experience.

NOTE: This futuristic sketch has been developed on the theory that a figment of the imagination has a good chance of spawning a teaspoon of practicality.

Chapter 15

Passing Your School Referendum: Community Support is Based on Credibility

by Patricia A. Myler, AIA

Gaining the support of the community to fund a school project is a challenging task, particularly in transitional economic times. A referendum campaign, much like a school building itself, has to be carefully designed, because success does not happen by accident. The time and energy invested in planning, organizing, and running a campaign will be rewarded with the support of the community and a positive referendum vote.

It has been our experience that a well-designed and implemented communications program and campaign plan goes a long way toward achieving that support. The following is an outline of the referendum campaign process as it should generally occur. This process has to be customized, however, to address the distinctive needs of a particular community.

DESIGNING THE CAMPAIGN

The Project Architect. The architect is a critically important member of the referendum campaign team. The school district needs the expertise and technical guidance of an architectural firm—one specializing in school design and construction—to prepare the necessary design and other documents for presentations and public forums. In addition, an experienced architecture firm can lead the whole team through the referendum process by sharing knowledge gained in similar referendums in other communities. This guidance is extremely important. The questions raised by the project's opponents, by its supporters, and by those voters who remain undecided must be answered professionally and completely to build the credibility necessary for victory.

Designing the Message. The target audience—those voters who are pro-education—must be identified, understood, and their electoral strength assessed. Research must be done into past campaigns and town referendums to determine the number of votes needed to win. The campaign team should utilize public hearings, focus groups, and questionnaires to identify voter issues and concerns.

Strong, organized opposition is often the primary factor in defeating a referendum. It is therefore critical to identify who is against the project and to determine why they oppose it *and* what alternatives they might support. Proposals should be structured to neutralize the opposition's arguments and to minimize surprises by predicting their reaction.

The communications subcommittee has the difficult task of sorting through all the information gathered and selecting three or four key facts that address the voters' major questions and clearly differentiate the arguments in support of the proposal from those of the opposition. The message needs to be simple and consistently repeated for voters to absorb the information. The need for the project, the benefit it will bring to the community, alternative options offered for consideration, tax implications, and the problems raised by doing nothing—all these should be addressed as part of the message.

The members of the coalition committee—rather than the architect, district officials, or building committee members, who may be perceived to have a bias—should be the key deliverers of the message. Frequent coalition meetings will be required to coordinate the content of the message and ensure consistency in its delivery.

Timing. The campaign should be initiated at least two to three months before the scheduled referendum date. This period is needed to organize the coalition, design the campaign, and disseminate the necessary information to the voters. When the referendum is scheduled is extremely important to its success. The referendum should not coincide with municipal votes, nor should it occur during the summer months. During the summer, families with school-age children go on vacation, and low voter turnout—especially among those with the greatest stake in the project's success—can lead to defeat. Also, part-time summer residents may be less likely to support educational bond issues.

Getting the Message Out. The campaign has to determine the best mix of tools for communicating its message. A variety of communication tools are available, including paid advertising (print and broadcast), free media, direct mail, telephone banks, literature drops, neighborhood "walk and talks," public speaking, and letters to the editor.

Available resources will vary, but they can include volunteers, private funding, and business donations of materials, phone banks, meeting space, and free advertising. The coalition committee must evaluate the available resources and develop a strategy to maximize their utilization.

Campaigns utilizing private funding are likely to be subject to strict regulation, and the coalition committee may even have to register as a political action committee (PAC). In most states, a guide to campaign financing is available from the state elections enforcement commission. There are also limitations on the role of public officials and consultants hired with public funds (including the architect) in the referendum process, and these must be fully understood to avoid conflict with these regulations.

The architect should prepare visual materials including site and floor plans, elevations, renderings, models, and CAD-generated animations. These graphic materials can be used in conjunction with a message developed to "tell the story." Posters and flyers can be developed for posting, mailing, and handing out. Local cable TV stations will provide free airtime to present the plans and animations and to broadcast discussions about the project. The campaign should also make the best use of press releases to local media, organize writing campaigns of letters to the editor, and sponsor public presentations and person-to-person neighborhood "walk and talks." The support of the local press is immensely valuable. Endorsements by local media gain votes.

Phone banks are another important communication tool. It is desirable to have a location with multiple phone lines. Here, volunteers can call voters who belong to the targeted segments and deliver a carefully scripted message. This tool can be utilized at the initiation of the campaign as an information-gathering exercise, and again later on to remind the pro-education voters to get out and vote. For a referendum in Watertown, Connecticut, a major corporation donated the use of its facility as a weekly meeting place for the coalition and as a phone bank location. This support from a local business saved the coalition a large amount of money and provided a central rallying location.

IMPLEMENTING THE CAMPAIGN

Phase 1: Educating the Voter. The education phase of a referendum process is a necessary first step. This phase brings issues within the school district to the public's attention, thus establishing "the need".

Establishing the Need. It is essential that the needs are established and communicated in order to solicit community support for a potential solution. It is equally important for the school district to understand the perceptions of their customers, (administrators, teachers, parents, students, community, and the taxpayers). There must be an up-front commitment to understand these customers' points of view before any attempt is made to engage their support.

Demographic Research. Questionable demographic research can lead to diminished support for public education. The shrinking market of school-aged children in the late 1960s and early 1970s led to school closures in many communities. With schools either closed or outdated there is a shortage of classroom and learning space. The public's recollection of this history must be addressed when projects are put forth for renovations, additions or new schools. The proper demographic research must be executed to establish a credible database for future planning.

Community Relations. The public school's relationship with the public or their customers does not begin with the development of the referendum process. Schools must develop and implement a long-range approach to optimize the daily interactions with their customers, and to solidify a supportive and informed contingency. Perceptions of a school or an entire district cannot be reversed within a relatively short referendum campaign. These beliefs about a school system, whether or not accurate or deserved, can account for much of what happens inside the voter booth.

Phase 2: The Campaign—Get the Story Out! Getting the story out to voters begins with a referendum workshop, or campaign kickoff meeting, in which the campaign process is defined and the design of the campaign plan is initiated.

During this initial meeting, the campaign leadership positions are identified and the associated responsibilities defined. Appointments are made to each of the following campaign leadership positions:

- Campaign Chairperson

- Volunteer Coordinators for Research, Neighborhood Distribution, Phone Banks, and Business Support

- Communications Coordinator

Subcommittees are established to work with each campaign leader, and volunteers sign up for subcommittees. Assignments are made to initiate the research tasks for each subcommittee. The schedule and tasks are reviewed for production of a detailed campaign plan.

Table 15.1 presents the duties of the campaign chairperson and each of the volunteer coordinators.

15.1. Campaign Leadership Positions

Title	Responsibilities
I. Campaign Chairperson	1. Serves as chief spokesperson for the campaign.
	2. Administers the agreed-upon campaign plan.
	3. Chairs the Campaign Leadership Committee.
II. Volunteer Coordinators	
Research Coordinator	1. Researches targeted pr-education groups, including parents', PTA, and community groups. Cross-references target groups against voter registration lists.
	2. Researches past referendum results.
Neighborhood Distribution Coordinator	1. Identifies most effective neighborhood drop locations.
	2. Identifies most effective public distribution areas.
	3. Organizes and coordinates volunteers for the activities above.
	4. Coordinates timing of activities with the campaign plan.
Phone Bank Coordinator	1. Arranges for phone bank location(s).
	2. Organizes and coordinates volunteers for phone bank(s). Coordinates volunteers with the Neighborhood Distribution subcommittee.
	3. Coordinates timing of activities with the campaign plan.
Business Support Coordinator	1. Solicits support of local business.
	2. Coordinates placement of posters and flyers with the campaign plan.
III. Communication Coordinators	
Community Presentations Coordinator	1. Coordinates community presentations with the campaign plan.
	2. Designs presentations to incorporate the campaign plan.
Message Development Coordinator	1. Works with subcommittee to develop and refine key messages to be incorporated into campaign plan.
	2. Plans and develops press releases, reflecting the key messages.
Letters to the Editor Coordinator	1. Develops letter drafts based on the key campaign messages.
	2. Organizes and coordinates volunteers for letter-writing.
	3. Coordinates timing of letter placement with campaign plan.

Part IV: Issues

Table 15.2. shows how you might design a volunteer sign-up sheet for the various subcommittees.

Table 15.2. Sample Subcommittee Sign-Up Sheet

Please check off the subcommittee you would be interested in working on.

			Research	Neighborhood Distribution	Phone Bank
Name	Telephone	Email	Chairperson: ___	Chairperson: ___	Chairperson: ___

Table 15.3. presents a sample schedule for two-month (March / April) campaign for a referendum scheduled for early May.

Table 15.3. Campaign Schedule

Task	3/3	3/10	3/17	3/24	3/31	4/07	4/14	4/21	4/28	5/5
Community Presentations										
Develop list										
Neighborhood Drops										
Message 1										
Message 2										
Message 3										
Message 4										
Message 5										
Public Distribution										
Letters to the Editor										
Draft letters										
Message 1										
Message 2										
Message 3										
Message 4										
Message 5										
Press Releases										
School Tour										
Cable TV Show										
Phone Bank										
Call pro-ed voters										
Research										
Identify pro-ed target										
Compare voter list										
ID opposition message										
Develop Campaign Message										
Flyers										
Posters										
Other Campaign Materials*										

* Other campaign materials might include poster boards for presentations (including floor plans, elevations), models, PowerPoint presentations, computer-generated video fly-through, etc.

Once the campaign plan has been developed, volunteers have signed up, and the schedule has been set, it's time to begin implementing the campaign. Some of the steps you'll need to follow are:

Step 1: Identify the Target Groups and Assess Their Electoral Strength

- Research past campaigns and town referendums. Based on past referendum history, establish the number of votes needed to win (50 percent of the number likely to vote plus 1).

- Identify the target groups or voter segments most likely to support the referendum.

- Identify undecided and opponent voters.

- To determine the electoral strength of the target group, transfer lists of voters likely to support the referendum to the voting lists. This crossed-referenced list will serve as the basis for designing the communications program.

- Call identified "yes" voters.

- Maintain up-to-date voting records.

Step 2: Design an Effective Campaign Message

- Find out what the voters think and what they want to know. Based on feedback from public forums, newspaper articles and editorials, surveys, and general discussions, develop a list of the most important questions, issues, and concerns.

- Differentiate the arguments of the opposition. Determine who opposes the project and why they oppose it and what they might support as an alternative. Structure the proposal to neutralize the opponents' arguments and to minimize surprises by predicting the opponents' reactions.

- Keep the message simple and concise. Select three or four key facts that address the voters' major questions. The simple, concise message needs to be repeated consistently in order for voters to absorb the information.

Step 3: Determine the Mix of Tools to Communicate the Campaign Message

- Select communications tools based on the number of votes needed to win and their location, the message being communicated, and the availability of resources, (final and human).

You may want to use any or all of the following communications tools:

- Paid advertising—print and broadcast

- Paid advertising—outdoor media

- Free media

- Direct mail

- Phone banks

- Mailers

- Flyers

- Newsletters

- Press releases

- Press interviews

- Press conferences with TV, radio, newspapers

- Student participation

- Tours through existing, inadequate facilities

- Literature drops

- Neighborhood "walks and talks"

- Letters to the editor

- Public presentations to different groups (including the board of education, PTA/PTO, general public, students, media, town council)

- Email bursts

- A referendum website

Conclusion:

Looking Ahead

About the future one can never say the final word. And so this conclusion isn't a "conclusion" (in the sense of something final) at all. The only sensible way to "conclude" a book about the future is to look ahead, with openness, to the changes the future will bring.

In the years ahead, Americans will continue to focus on the nature and quality of our public education system, debating and experimenting with ways of strengthening the educational experience we give our children and improving the preparation they receive for entering the worlds of college, work, adult relationships, parenting, and citizenship. To accommodate new educational technologies and new approaches to schooling (undoubtedly including some that we cannot now predict), we must design schools to be as flexible as possible. But it's equally clear that our own thinking about what flexibility *is* and how it can best be achieved must also continue to evolve.

To respond effectively to the changes the future may bring, we must ourselves be willing to change our thinking, our strategies, and our priorities. This is a potentially endless task, and one that we—as designers, educators, parents, and citizens—should welcome. In concluding this book, we look forward to publishing further editions, in which the thinking we express here is refined, corrected, augmented, expanded—*changed* in ways that address the ongoing changes in American education, society, and culture.

We believe that our long experience in designing the full range of public education facilities provides us with insights that may be of value to middle school, high school, specialized school, and community college educators and administrators, as well. The other books in the Schools of the Future series are intended to serve these audiences: *The Elementary School of the Future* and *The Middle School of the Future* are being published simultaneously with this volume; *Magnet and Charter Schools of the Future* and *Community Colleges of the Future* will appear in 2004 and 2005, respectively.

Finally, we mean what we say, throughout this book, when we speak of the value of collaboration and democratic process in school planning, design, and construction. It's our consistent experience as designers that thinking gets better and solutions become more effective as participation in the design process widens and grows. We therefore invite you, our readers, to participate in the making of future editions of this book. If there's anything you wish to respond to—anything we've missed, or overemphasized, or gotten wrong (or gotten right)—we'd very much like to hear from you. Contact us through our website, <www.fletcherthompson.com>.

gets better and solutions become more effective as participation in the design process widens and grows. We therefore invite you, our readers, to participate in the making of future editions of this book. If there's anything you wish to respond to—anything we've missed, or overemphasized, or gotten wrong (or gotten right)—we'd very much like to hear from you.

Contact us through our website, **<www.fletcherthompson.com>, by phone (203/366-5441) or fax (203/339-6444),** or by writing to us: Educational Studio, Fletcher-Thompson, Inc., Two Lafayette Square, Bridgeport, CT 06604-3944.

Sources Cited

Department of Education, State of Connecticut. 2000. "The New Connecticut High School: Re-Defining Graduation Requirements." Draft monograph. October 16. N.p.

Dhar, Vasant, and Roger Stein. 1997. *Seven Methods for Transforming Corporate Data into Business Intelligence.* Englewood Cliffs, N.J.: Prentice-Hall.

Dillon, Sam. 2002. "Heft of Students' Backpacks Turns Into Textbook Battle." *New York Times.* December 24.

Gross, Jane. 2003. "What's Big, Yellow and Humiliating? Full Lot at Greenwich High Means New Reality: The Bus." *New York Times.* January 27.

Hirshberg, Jerry. 1998. *The Creative Priority: Driving Innovative Business in the Real World.* New York: HarperBusiness.

IBM. 1997. "Data Management Customer Solutions and Success." Website: www.ibm.com.

Inmon, W. H. 1996. *Building the Data Warehouse.* 2d ed. New York: John Wiley & Sons.

Pinker, Steven. 2003. "How to Get Inside a Student's Head." *New York Times.* January 31.

Simon, Alan R. 1997. *Data Warehousing for Dummies.* Foster City, Calif.: IDG Books Worldwide.

Sterling, Bruce. 2002. *Tomorrow Now: Envisioning the Next Fifty Years.* New York: Random House.

Winter, Greg. 2003. "Gates Foundation Providing $31 Million for Small Schools." *New York Times.* February 26.

Online Resources:

A Selected List

- The Connecticut Academy for Education publishes a useful online list of educational technology-related websites. www.ctacad.org/Internet/default.htm

- The Council of Educational Facilities Planners, International, publishes an annual directory, accessible online, of educational facilities consultants. www.cefpi.org

- "An Educator's Guide to Evaluating the Use of Technology in Schools and Classrooms (December 1998)," though slightly out of date, remains valuable. www.ed.gov/pubs/EdTechGuide/

- "Electronic Collaboration: A Practical Guide for Educators" is a downloadable PDF document from the LAB at Brown (the Northeast and Islands Regional Educational Laboratory at Brown University); it features an 11-step process for making online collaborative projects successful. www.lab.brown.edu/public/pubs/collab/elec-collab.pdf

- The George Lukas Educational Foundation produces regular newsletters on the latest trends in K-12 facilities. http://glef.org

- "The Impact of Educational Technology on Student Achievement: What the Most Current Research Has to Say" is a downloadable PDF document from the Milken Exchange on Educational Technology. www.milkenexchange.org/project/research/ME161.pdf

- "K-12 Educational Resources" is a thorough list of online resources pertaining to education and technology; from the Technology Education Lab. www.techedlab.com/k12.html

- The Learning Research and Development Center of the University of Pittsburgh has a useful website that includes information on learning and technology. www.lrdc.pitt.edu

- STaR (School Technology and Readiness) Charts, published by the CEO Forum on Education and Technology, are self-assessment tools designed to help schools, teachers' colleges, and departments of education assess how well prepared teachers are to use technology. www.ceoforum.org

- "Tales from the Electronic Frontier" shares how teachers have integrated technology into math and science curriculums; it includes a list of websites addressing technology issues, tools, resources, and projects. www.wested.org/tales/

- "Valiant, Etc." is a website that's chock-full of "News and Resources for Thoughtful Educators." www.valetc.com

- "Tales from the Electronic Frontier" shares how teachers have integrated technology into math and science curriculums; it includes a list of websites addressing technology issues, tools, resources, and projects. www.wested.org/tales/

- "Valiant, Etc." is a website that's chock-full of "News and Resources for Thoughtful Educators." www.valetc.com

Contributors

Edwin T. Merritt, Ed.D., is Director of Educational Planning & Research for Fletcher-Thompson, Inc. Over his 29-year career as a school superintendent (in three different districts), Ted Merritt was involved in more than 25 new construction, renovation, and major maintenance projects. A futurist and an expert on educational technology, he currently serves as a consultant on technology planning for the Connecticut State Department of Education. Mr. Merritt has received many awards, including the Connecticut State Superintendents' Golden Shield Award for Exemplary Service (1999), the General Connecticut Coast YMCA "Strong Kids Builder" Award (1999), the Bridgeport Regional Leader of the Year Award (1998), and the Rotary Club's Paul Harris Fellowship (1998), and he has been a National and State Parent/Teachers' Association Honoree (1993, 1999). He has written for *American School & University* and *School Business Affairs,* among other publications.

James A. Beaudin, AIA, is the Principal of Fletcher-Thompson, Inc.'s Education Practice Group. Over his career, Mr. Beaudin has been involved in the design of almost 100 schools in 45 communities—for a total of more than 10 million square feet of public and private school construction. Since 1990, the firm, under his direction, has created more than 7.5 million square feet of educational space, with a combined construction value in excess of $500 million and comprising projects for every educational level, from pre-kindergarten through high school. Besides new construction, projects directed by Mr. Beaudin have included renovations, code-compliance improvements, system-wide studies, and educational programming and specification development. Under his leadership, Fletcher Thompson's Education Practice Group has received numerous awards and other recognition. Articles authored or co-authored by Mr. Beaudin have appeared in *American School & University, Facilities Design & Management, School Business Affairs,* and *School Planning & Management* magazines.

Jeffrey A. Sells, AIA, is the Design Leader of Fletcher-Thompson, Inc.'s Education Practice Group, responsible for the design approach on all of the firm's educational projects. He has designed new elementary and high school buildings as well as additions and renovations of elementary, middle, high, and magnet schools in districts throughout Connecticut. He has also designed college and university facilities, including the Thomas Dodd Archives and Research Center at the University of Connecticut. His work has been featured in professional publications and has won numerous awards and special recognition. His written work has appeared in *Engineering News-Record, School Business Affairs, American School and University,* and *The CABE Journal,* and he has been a collaborator on, or primary contributor to, articles for *Contract* and *Building Design & Construction* magazines and the *Connecticut Post.*

Richard S. Oja, AIA, is a Senior Project Manager at Fletcher-Thompson, Inc. For more than 12 years, he has managed public school projects, from project inception through programming, design, bidding, construction, and post-occupancy evaluation. He has worked on a full range of educational facilities, from small elementary schools to major suburban and urban high schools. He has focused on schools' indoor environmental quality issues, giving presentations and publishing articles, including a recent piece in *Facilities Design & Management,* on the topic.

Patricia A. Myler, AIA, is Director of Pre-K through Grade 12 Facilities and an Associate at Fletcher-Thompson, Inc. Since joining the firm in 1995, she has served as a studio leader and project manager and is currently Director of the firm's Hartford, Connecticut, office, focusing on educational projects that have ranged from feasibility studies for elementary, middle, high, and magnet schools; to additions and renovations; to new primary, magnet, middle, and high schools. She has also provided pre-referendum consulting services to several Connecticut school districts. She is the co-author of a recent *School Business Affairs* article, "Going Up?," on the feasibility of vertical expansions of existing school facilities.

Marcia T. Palluzzi, LA, is registered landscape architect. While she was at Fletcher-Thompson, Inc., her work focused on the pre-planning process, programming, land-use studies, and regulatory approvals for educational and other projects.

Photo Credits